A
CHICANO
THEOLOGY

ANDRÉS G. GUERRERO

ORBIS BOOKS

Maryknoll, New York 10545

The Catholic Foreign Mission Society of America (Maryknoll) recruits and trains people for overseas missionary service. Through Orbis Books Maryknoll aims to foster the international dialogue that is essential to mission. The books published, however, reflect the opinions of their authors and are not meant to represent the official position of the society.

Library of Congress Cataloging-in-Publication Data

Guerrero, Andrés Gonzales.

  A Chicano theology.

  Bibliography: p.
  Includes index.
  1. Liberation theology.   2. Mexican Americans—
Social conditions.   3. Mexican Americans—Religion.
4. Guadalupe, Our Lady of.   5. Vasconcelos, José,
1882–1959.   Raza cósmica.   I. Title.
BT83.57.G84   1986   230′.0896872073   86-23561
ISBN 0-88344-407-0 (pbk.)

Contents

Acknowledgments

I dedicate this book to Juanita, my esteemed companion and friend, who worked very hard to help me complete it. I owe special thanks to Andrés III, Miguel, Raquel, and Gabriel, our children.

I want to acknowledge the assistance of Professor Harvey Cox, who inspired the title and method of this thesis; Professor Marie Augusta Neal, S.N.D., whose encouragement helped me so much; Professor George Thompson, Jr., for his moral support; and Professor Nancy Jay, whose unceasing labor, critical comments, and dedication helped me clarify what I had taken for granted.

I acknowledge the poor, *los pobres*, who will inherit the earth just as Christ prophesied they would. It is the Christian duty of the teacher and theologian to be at their side as it happens.

I thank our parents, Andrés and Guadalupe, Benito and Nieves, our brothers and sisters, and all our family and friends, whose support, encouragement, and inspiration helped bring these studies to fruition.

Last, but by no means least, *nuestras muchísimas gracias* to all the Chicano leaders who shared their ideas, visions, and hopes for the Chicano community. In their struggle for the liberation of our Chicano community, may God and *Nuestra Señora de Guadalupe* grant them the strength, warmth, and peace they need to accomplish this necessary task.

Introduction

For one hundred and thirty years we Chicanos have been under-represented and virtually voiceless in the social, economic, political, and spiritual decisions that have determined our destiny. This book is a study of our sociohistorical and ecclesiastical situation. It is also an investigation of the symbolic role of *Nuestra Señora de Guadalupe* and of the notion of *La Raza Cósmica* in understanding the Chicano cosmic-universal experience of oppression and in developing a Chicano theology of liberation.

Part 1 outlines the Chicano sociohistorical and ecclesiastical written tradition (chapters 1 and 2) and serves as an introduction for the reader to the Chicano oral tradition, which is explored in Part 2 (chapter 3). The first chapter presents a brief history of the Chicanos in the Southwest. Fray Bartolomé de Las Casas and Padre José Antonio Martínez exemplify the two conquests described in this chapter. Chapter 2 examines the Chicano cosmic experience of oppression.

Part 2 begins by exploring the Chicano oral tradition through interviews with nine Chicano leaders (two women and seven men). Chapter 3 consists of a synthesis of the interviews with these leaders, who give in-depth responses to several issues that oppress our people. These persons were chosen because of their commitment and dedication to the Chicano community. I shared with them twelve themes dealing with economic, political, social, cultural, and spiritual questions in our lives. They expressed their opinions about the Chicano situation in an open setting and suggested some solutions toward our liberation. This information is important because it is not found in libraries. It is part of our oral tradition.

Chapter 4 analyzes the symbol of Guadalupe as it pertains to the Chicano situation. Chapter 5 analyzes the symbol of *La Raza Cósmica*. It is a symbol of the pride we feel in being identified as

1

Chicano and in combatting the milieu of oppression in which Chicanos are stereotyped as inferiors.

Chapter 6 sets out some conclusions and perspectives. It first identifies the poor (*los pobres*). It states that the Magnificat provides a theological base for Guadalupe as she provides for us a sociological vision of a new humanity—a vision in which the mighty are brought down and the lowly are raised up. Luke's announcement of the good news (4:18–19) is a message of liberation to the oppressed. Oppressed Chicanos, with their folk Catholicism, respond to this message by nurturing the symbol of Guadalupe and asking for her intercession.

This chapter explores the symbolic roles of *Nuestra Señora de Guadalupe* and *La Raza Cósmica* in the development of a Chicano theology of liberation. Both are symbols that unify us and give cosmic order and hope to our situation of oppression. Both relate to the Lukan message of the good news of liberation to the oppressed.

Finally, this last chapter sets out the essential elements of a Chicano theology of liberation as derived from an analysis of the experiences of the Chicano leaders interviewed. A Chicano theology of liberation ought not to support in any way elements or acts or theories that are racist, sexist, anti-Semitic, or classist. The heart (*el corazón*) of its content ought to be in the context of the Lukan message of the good news to the poor.

My study reinforces the significance of Guadalupe and *La Raza Cósmica* as symbols that give Chicanos a sense of cosmic-universal order and that tie us to the global community. Both symbols, Guadalupe and *La Raza Cósmica*, will be instrumental in developing our theology and in giving it a social vision.

PART 1

Historical Perspectives on the Chicano Cosmic Experience of Oppression

CHAPTER 1

A Brief History of Chicanos

Conquest is at the ground of Chicano history. Two major conquests stand out. The first conquest was by the Spaniards in the sixteenth century; the second by the gringos[1] in the nineteenth century. The history and personal identity of the Chicanos is shaped by these two conquests. Both conquests were so brutal that they left unforgettable memories upon the conquered. In a sense Chicanos are a by-product of these two historical conflicts.

The roots of Chicano history are in the sixteenth century conquest, when two cultures, two world views, and two world powers —the indigenous and the Spanish—merged violently. The Spanish conquistador married or raped the conquered Indian woman. The children born of this union were neither indigenous nor Spanish. Thus began a new race (*La Raza*), which had characteristics of both groups. At first these children had a difficult time; both groups rejected them. Neither the Spanish nor the indigenous wanted them. The Spaniards labeled these children *mestizos*—a mixture of Spanish and indigenous. This phenomenon of the New World was called *mestizaje*. This was not the first time *mestizaje* had occurred however.[2]

From the beginning, these people had two names. The Spaniards called them *mestizos*; they called themselves *La Raza*. Both names mean the same thing. Today, Chicanos are *mestizos* and they call themselves *La Raza*. Chicano is the name we gave ourselves after the second conquest in the nineteenth century by the gringos. After this second conquest the gringo called us Mexican-American—a hyphenated name. Clearly put, we are Chicanos who are *mestizos* and members of *La Raza*. Some members of *La Raza* prefer to be called Mexican-American because the term *Chicano* is associated with militancy.

During the first conquest, the institution that was instrumental in bringing to reality the *mestizo* phenomenon was the Catholic Church. Once native Americans were baptized, they were Christians and fell under the jurisdiction and protection of the church's laws. Under the church's sacraments, Spaniards and native Americans, more positively this time, intermarried. In principle (thanks to the church), there was equality, but not in practice.

After the second conquest what had been almost half of Mexico's territory became the American Southwest. For a second time, we were a people conquered by outsiders. Once more a church with an alien clergy (the native clergy was ousted or repressed) continued its sacramental tradition among the *mestizos*. *Mestizos* had resided in the Southwest since the Spanish conquest. They had built churches and sophisticated mission systems throughout the Southwest. In California, Texas, and New Mexico the church was strong and powerful. The native Americans and the *mestizos* were oppressed but they managed to survive and sometimes to thrive, thanks to the church.

I believe that the *mestizo* has survived as *La Raza* in the United States because of the Catholic Church. I say this because the second conquest occurred in the midst of America's belief in its Manifest Destiny, in the midst of the displacement and genocide of native Americans, which would continue into the twentieth century.

Attempts by Protestant clergy to defend the native Americans were not as successful. When the Cherokees were driven from their lands, they left a "trail of tears" on their journey to Oklahoma. The missionaries of the Protestant churches, especially from New England, tried to stop the displacement but to no avail. Protestant ministers suffered prison terms, displacement, broken families, and other calamities at the hands of state officials. But their political power was not strong enough to stop the removal and genocide of the native American.

Unlike the native American, the Chicano population was not obliterated by genocidal practices. The nation of *mestizos* in Mexico was willing to migrate into the United States (still spiritually and psychologically their own land) to replace Chicanos who had been killed by gringos. Today, Chicanos are the largest group of Hispanos in the United States. Together with the other Hispano groups they comprise about 35 percent of the Catholic population in the United States.

One historical figure from each period of conquest will serve to elucidate Chicano issues of race and class, social, economic, political, and spiritual oppression.

An analysis of Fray Bartolomé de Las Casas will capture the spirit of the first conquest; Padre Antonio José Martínez, the second conquest. I have chosen these two men to exemplify the two conquests because of their dedication to the struggle of the oppressed.

FRAY BARTOLOMÉ DE LAS CASAS: OPPRESSOR AND LIBERATOR

Fray Bartolomé de Las Casas, a bishop, a historian, and a political theorist, was not always a defender of native Americans. When Las Casas first set foot in the New World, he was an ecclesiastic and an *encomendero*. The theory of the *encomienda* was simple. The Spanish gave or "commended" Indians to Spaniards, who became *encomenderos*; this grant gave the Spaniards the right to exact labor or tribute from the Indians. In return the *encomenderos* were obligated to provide religious instruction for their Indians and to protect them.[3]

Las Casas graduated from the University of Salamanca and shortly after was ordained a priest. He came to the New World, like all the conquistadores, to gain fame and fortune. It was probably in 1502 that he arrived from Spain in the New World.[4] In 1512 he participated in the conquest of Cuba and received as a reward both land and the service of some Indians.[5]

We must say that the first relationship Las Casas had with the native Americans was as an oppressor. His conversion to fighting for the rights of native Americans began when he was forty years old. For the remaining fifty years of his life he would defend them, first as a Dominican friar, then as a bishop, and finally as a scholar.

Las Casas was responsible for introducing Black slavery into the New World. Later he saw that slavery was slavery, no matter the color of a person's skin. The slavery of any human being could not be justified because of its brutality and indignity to men and women.

Las Casas's conversion from oppressor to liberator began on the Third Sunday of Advent, November 30, 1511. A Dominican, Friar Antonio de Montesinos, approached the pulpit in Hispañola (Cuba). His sermon was almost as devastating as the Spanish conquest had been. The difference was that it was directed against the Spaniards and was in defense of the native Americans. The church had taken a stand. Las Casas tells us how Montesinos's sermon began:

> I am the voice of one crying in the wilderness of this island; it behooves you to listen with attention and not just any attention, but with the attention of your heart and all your senses; hear it, which voice will be the most new you have ever heard, the most harsh, most difficult, and most frightful and dangerous you have ever thought of hearing.[6]

Fray Montesinos continued:

> By what law and by what justice do you hold these Indians under such horrible and cruel conditions? By what authority have you waged such detestable wars upon these people who are in their own gentle and peaceful lands, so infinitely theirs, with deaths and ravages never heard of before, you have devastated. How do you keep them so oppressed and so exhausted without giving them something to eat, not curing them of their infirmities which from the excessive work you give them they incur and eventually die; or better said, you kill for the sake of taking out and acquiring gold every day? And what care have you taken to teach them doctrine, to know God their Creator, to be baptized, to hear Mass, to hear music, and to keep feastdays and Sundays? These, are they not men? Have they not rational souls? Are you not to love them as you love yourselves? Do you not understand this? Do you not feel this? How can you be in such profound unawareness, so lethargically asleep? Bear for certain that in the state in which you are, you cannot be more saved than the

Moors or Turks who do not have nor want the faith of Jesus Christ.[7]

When Montesinos was asked to recant his sermon, his response the following week to the prominent political figures in the community was even more devastating than his first sermon had been. Montesinos quoted from the Book of Job.

> Elihu also proceeded and said:
> Suffer me a little, and I will show thee:
> for I have yet somewhat to speak in God's behalf.
> I will repeat my knowledge from the beginning
> And I will prove my maker just.
> For indeed My words are without a lie
> And perfect knowledge shall be proved to thee
> [Job 36:1–4, DV].

From the tone of his sermon, it would be reasonable to believe that Montesinos would not recant. He went on to speak at the court of Spain on behalf of the Indians and eventually met his death while protecting them in Venezuela.[8]

Montesinos's sermon would stay in Las Casas's mind for two years before he changed his way of life. One day in 1514, while preparing a sermon, Las Casas came across these verses in Ecclesiasticus.[9]

> The sacrifice of an offering unjustly acquired is a mockery;
>   the gifts of impious men are unacceptable.
> The Most High takes no pleasure in offerings from the godless,
>   multiplying sacrifices will not gain his pardon for sin.
> Offering sacrifice from the property of the poor
>   is as bad as slaughtering a son before his father's very eyes
>   [Ecclus 34:18–20, JB].

As Las Casas read the passage, he could not forget that he was an *encomendero*; therefore, his offering was a mockery. Because he was an *encomendero* there was no way God could accept his offering. This passage must have affected him especially because he was a priest. Daily he offered the Sacrifice of the Mass. Even this supreme sacrifice was in jeopardy of being rejected.

All this was more than Las Casas could bear. He experienced a metanoia. He finally chose to fight for the native American, who was held in bondage by the Spaniards.

According to Las Casas, the *encomienda* system was destroying the native Americans; it was an unjust and tyrannical system. For Las Casas, Montesinos had been prophetic in his analysis. The Spaniards were wrong in their enslavement and treatment of the native American. But Las Casas went even further than Montesinos. For him the whole conquest had been an unjust and tyrannical act: "All wars called conquests were and are most unjust and truly tyrannical."[10] He further contended that native Americans had the right to make just war against the Spaniards and that this right would be theirs until the Day of Judgment.[11]

So spoke Bartolomé de Las Casas to kings and popes and other political powers. He had inherited Montesinos's charisma to defend the native Americans. He disproved before the court of Spain the Aristotelian theory that was used to support the contention that by nature the native Americans were slaves. Furthermore he began and institutionalized a method of attracting all peoples to the Christian faith.[12] This method for converting people stressed the use of peaceful means rather than brute force. He proved by his own ministry to the native Americans that this method worked. He wanted Spain to colonize the New World by sending men and women to farm the land instead of exploiting the native Americans and mining for gold and silver. Colonization did not work because the Spaniards who did come came to gain fame and seek fortune.

Las Casas will always have a special place in the history of the Americas. He fought within the institutional framework of the Catholic Church, and his endeavors for the liberation of the oppressed native Americans in Central and South America prevented their being decimated as the native Americans in the West Indies and in North America were.

THE TREATY OF GUADALUPE-HIDALGO

The historical figure who captures the spirit of the second conquest is Padre Antonio José Martínez. Before analyzing the life of Padre Martínez, we must consider the Treaty of Guadalupe-

Hidalgo. In Chicano history this treaty marks the transition between the first and the second conquests.

The Treaty of Guadalupe-Hidalgo, signed by the United States and Mexico, ended the Mexican-American War in 1848. The United States was given half of all the territory of Mexico, today's American Southwest. Within the territory handed over to the United States lived several thousand Mexican citizens. After one year, according to this treaty, these Mexican citizens could either remain in the occupied territory and become United States citizens or they could leave the conquered territory and remain Mexican citizens. According to Articles VIII, IX, and X (a Protocol was substituted for Article X) Mexicans would receive the protection of the United States government in the exercise of their civil and political rights.[13] Land grants and property rights were to be honored by the new government. After the treaty was signed, the gringo political and military forces who occupied the Southwest reinforced the psychological, social, and economic captivity of the Chicanos.

The United States did not keep its treaty with Mexico. Many Chicanos suffered brutally under the gringo yoke after 1848. None of the demands for the protection of the Chicanos who stayed on their land was honored. Fraud, deceit, illegal taxation practices, lying, and cheating caused the Chicanos to lose their property within twelve years after the treaty was signed. The army of occupation situated itself strategically in order to insure that Chicanos remained poor, illiterate, landless, and without any representative rights whatsoever.[14] Chicanos were to be captive strangers in their own land.

Since the United States made a mockery of the treaty when it came to the protection of the Chicanos, the Chicanos had to fend for themselves if they were to survive. I might add that Chicanos were not the first to experience broken treaties with the United States government.[15]

PADRE ANTONIO JOSÉ MARTÍNEZ: A NATIVE NEW MEXICAN RESISTER FOR THE OPPRESSED

The spiritual conquest of the Southwest was to be insured too. The native Mexican clergy had the choice of capitulating to a new foreign bishop, departing for Mexican territory, or leaving the church.

Padre Antonio José Martínez exemplifies the struggle of this time. As pastor of Our Lady of Guadalupe parish in Taos, New Mexico, he had been given senior authority by Bishop Zubiria of Durango over the priests in New Mexico. Padre Martínez was born in the mission parish of Santo Tomás in Abiquiu, New Mexico.[16]

There were several careers in the life of Antonio José Martínez, and perhaps that is what marks him as a great man.[17] At the same time that he was a busy pastor, he was also a publisher, educator, and political leader.[18] The first printing press west of the Mississippi was purchased by Padre Martínez.[19] He published books, pamphlets, and a newspaper called *El Crepúsculo de La Libertad*. In 1843, he had translated from Latin to Spanish some of the more important principles of civil law and printed them in a booklet called *Civil Rights*.[20] Padre Martínez saw the great need for higher education and training in the professions, particularly the priesthood and law, and he took steps to meet the challenge. When he approached Bishop Zubiria about training seminarians, the bishop told him of the financial difficulty of sending seminarians to study so far away from home. Padre Martínez decided to set up a Latin School to give preparatory training to his own seminarians.[21] This he did in 1833. In 1835, three seminarians were sent to Durango, where later they were ordained.[22]

About thirty students from Padre Martínez's schools were ordained to priesthood, most of them by Bishop Zubiria in Durango and four by Bishop Lamy.[23] These figures show the extent to which the native New Mexican clergy was developing before the arrival of the French bishop who was named vicar *in partibus infidelium*, vicar in "the regions of the infidels."[24] The American hierarchy and Rome considered the region of New Mexico a region of infidels.

Martínez also saw the need to defend his people in legal matters; so he established a law school with the hope that some of his students would study law to help the poor achieve justice.[25] Martínez had prepared himself by studying both civil and ecclesiastical statutes. He knew canon law and he knew Mexican and American law as well. Martínez loved freedom and hated oppression. He consistently opposed measures both in civil society and in the church that infringed upon the liberty of the people.[26]

So Padre Martínez was an educator, a publisher, a lawyer, a political leader, and a priest. He trained future priests and future lawyers. In spite of all this he was excommunicated by the French Bishop Lamy. Lamy wanted Padre Martínez to obey his authority; Martínez challenged it. Lamy wanted to reinstitute tithing, which had been outlawed by Mexican law in 1833,[27] but Martínez told Lamy that he could not do it, as it would be at the expense of the poor. Martínez took great pride in his successful campaign to abolish church tithing imposed by Mexican civil law.[28]

Even Bishop Zubiria had defended Padre Martínez in this political issue of tithing by affirming that Padre Martínez had "every right to express his opinions."[29] When Lamy re-instituted tithing, Padre Martínez wrote a letter to the editor of *La Gaceta* in Santa Fe re-stating his long time opposition to Church tithes. In a letter to Bishop Purcell of Cincinnati, Lamy interpreted the resistance to tithing as a boycott or embargo designed to force him out of the area.[30] Lamy responded with a second pastoral on January 14, 1854:

> Any family who does not support the Church [materially] will not have the right to receive the holy sacraments. Let us again inform you that we consider those as not belonging to the Church who do not observe this precept; and we likewise would take away all faculties to say Mass and administer the sacraments from all pastors who fail to sustain and provide for the maintenance of religion and its ministers.[31]

For two more years Padre Martínez resisted Bishop Lamy's tithing position. Finally, he decided to retire at the age of sixty-four. In January 1856 he asked Bishop Lamy to appoint Ramón Medina, a newly ordained Mexican-American priest, in his place. Four months later, May 5, 1856, Bishop Lamy appointed Damasio Taladrid, a Spaniard, an unpopular choice for the New Mexicans of Taos. On May 8, 1856, Padre Martínez presented his case to the people in a letter to the editor of *La Gaceta* in which he gave three reasons for his "resignation": his age, his worsening health, and the bishop's pastoral letter concerning taxes.[32]

As might be expected, Taladrid had a difficult time in Taos. On July 23 he reported to Lamy that Martínez was working on an article for *La Gaceta* concerning the abolition of tithes. It was published on September 3, 1856. Lucero, a friend and close associate of Padre Martínez, was suspended on September 29. Martínez, fearing that he would be next, wrote a letter to Bishop Lamy complaining about Father Taladrid and explaining his reasons for celebrating Mass in a private oratory. (On October 23, Taladrid had written to Bishop Lamy complaining that Padre Martínez was celebrating Mass in his private oratory.) Padre Martínez was suspended the following day.

On November 12, 1856, in a letter to Bishop Lamy, Padre Martínez tried to prove through canon law that the suspension was null and void.[33] He had never been cited or given a hearing or a trial as required by canon law. Padre Martínez in this letter reaffirmed his stand on tithing:

> Its total payment as you demand under most severe penalties is in violation of the rights of these my people among whom I first saw the light of day. . . . I beg your Excellency to respect my viewpoint for what I am about to say. . . . The diocesan statutes invite the faithful to enter into mercantile agreements making the parish priests appear like huskers or traders. They also make the sacraments, Masses, and other spiritual gifts as so much merchandise in a warehouse by order of Your Excellency. . . . Compare this way of acting with the account of Simon Magus in the Acts of the Apostles.[34]

Padre Martínez was to write five more letters to Bishop Lamy. He never received a reply. Four months later, Martínez reminded Lamy that he had been ignoring his letters. In reference to his suspension, Martínez called attention to Murillo's commentary on Canon Law (Vol. V. Sec. 31) *Decretals Against Bishops' Excesses in Matters of the Rights of their Clergy*. He informed Lamy that the Canonist Murrillo cited Pope Alexander III as his authority.[35]

One of those letters tells us something of what happened to the other New Mexican priests and how they were treated by Bishop Lamy. Padre Martínez wrote:

> Is it that you wished to treat me the way you treated and injured other priests who because of their candor suffered all

exactly the same way I do? What you did to Father Manuel Gallegos, the pastor of San Felipe, the church in Albuquerque, who because he had made a trip to Mexico in 1852 with due letters from the Vicar General returned to find himself suspended, his books and property thrown out of his rectory, and Father José Prospecto Machebeuf ensconced in his place. You did the same with the Vicar Forane, Father Juan Felipe Ortiz the next year without canonical regard, dividing his parish, taking his rectory away from him, and finally suspending him.[36]

The legal tone of these letters and the unjust manner in which Bishop Lamy treated the New Mexican priests lead one to suspect that the bishop was too angry to answer any of the letters. So Padre Martínez turned to the next in command, Father José Prospecto Machebeuf, the Vicar General. He pleaded with him not to destroy the peace and repose of his home and not to distress his faithful parishioners who came to him with their needs.[37] In the same letter Padre Martínez said:

> I recognize the duties which my conscience unfolds to me, as well as the help and consolation I have in Canon Law and in our liberal republican American Government in which I believe so confidently. These I feel will not allow the machinations of others to trouble me.[38]

In the same month, May of 1857, Lamy started formal procedures for excommunicating Padre Martínez. Lamy removed Taladrid from Taos and replaced him with Padre Eulogio Ortiz, a former pupil of Padre Martínez and the younger brother of the suspended priest, Padre Juan Felipe Ortiz. For Padre Martínez, joy turned sorrow when Padre Eulogio Ortiz implemented diocesan policies in regard to tithes and promoted uncritical loyalty to the bishop, whose secretary and traveling companion to Rome he had been.

Five months later Bishop Lamy excommunicated Padre Martínez. Padre Martínez and his followers from Taos were forced into schism. Martínez would remain separated from Bishop Lamy and steadfast to his position on tithing until his death seven years later.

CONCLUSION

The first conquest created *mestizaje*, a union of Spanish and indigenous. The Catholic Church was instrumental in sanctioning this union. *Mestizos* endured hardships because neither the Spanish nor the indigenous group wanted them. But as time passed the *mestizos* became the dominant group in Mexico. During this first conquest the *mestizos* adopted the name *La Raza*.

During this period Fray Bartolomé de Las Casas dedicated his life to the defense and survival of the indigenous native Americans. His writings tell us of the brutal devastation of the native Americans by the Spaniards. Las Casas was one of the first defenders of the oppressed in this hemisphere.

The second conquest by the gringos from the Northeast, which caused Mexico to lose half of its territory, was accomplished by the signing of the Treaty of Guadalupe-Hidalgo. The failure of the United States to honor the treaty insured the military occupation of Chicano lands in the Southwest. During this period, as exemplified by the experience of Padre Antonio José Martínez, even the church was against the Mexicans. The Mexican clergy was replaced by French and Spanish clergy. Padre Martínez resisted foreign influences and ecclesiastical policies that were unjust to the poor. The Chicano experience of oppression continued into the twentieth century because the Chicanos had no native clergy and because of the hierarchy's lack of social consciousness.

CHAPTER 2

The Chicano Cosmic Experience
of Oppression

PHENOMENA THAT CAPTURE THE CHICANO REALITY

Our *mestizo* ancestry is both Spanish and native American. Historically, then, we are both oppressor (Spanish) and oppressed (native American). Racially, we are both white (Spanish) and red (native American). Economically, the Spanish gained power as they acquired the land; native Americans lost power and became landless. We live in a gringo society, but our culture is Mexican. We have a gringo impulse (learned from the gringo), but our *corazón* is Latino. We relate to the impoverished world because of our oppression, but we live in a technological, industrial, affluent world. We embrace two world views in our reality, the European and the indigenous. We practice *machismo* (male chauvinism), yet our Mexican heritage is woman-centered. Our fathers are the heads of the household, but our mothers are the hearts of it. Some of us feel superior because we are white; some of us feel inferior because we are brown or red. The European in us is individually inclined; the indigenous in us is communally inclined. The Protestant in us is competitive, but the Catholic in us is social. As Protestants we have ecclesiastical leadership but lack social awareness; as Catholics we have a social consciousness, but little ecclesiastical leadership. The Jewish in us is exclusivistic; the Christian-Israelite in us is inclusivistic.[1] The following listing depicts the human dualities of our experience.

Common Experiences or Inheritances

A	B
Colonizer	Colonized
Spaniard	Native American
Oppressor	Oppressed
Landed	Landless
Gringo	Mexican
Superiority complex	Inferiority complex
Aztec priests and kings	Sacrificed victims
White	Brown/Red/Bronze
Power	Powerless
Affluent milieu	Impoverished milieu
Machismo	Female-centered culture
Individual	Communal
Exclusivistic	Inclusivistic
Foreigners	Natives
Rich	Poor
Competitive	Sharing
Gringo impulse	*Corazón Latino*
Protestant	Catholic
Jewish	Christian-Israelite
European Weltanschauung	Indigenous Weltanschauung
Institutional Catholicism	Folk Catholicism

Mixture of both

to

create

cosmic experience

Mix the contrasting phenomena listed—you really have to mix them in order to understand—and you have what we Chicanos call a "cosmic experience." I call it a cosmic experience of oppression. From this experience a theology of liberation for Chicanos has to be born. They are not easily found but I maintain that historical examples of committed individuals exist to show us the way (see chapter 3). Symbols also exist that tie us to the global community. This is essential if we are to find solutions to our problems as a global human family. It would be unreasonable to say that we have the solutions, or even a solution, but the Chicano experience of oppression and theology will give us insight leading to solutions. From their cosmic experience Chicanos will soon make their theological contribution.

THE WORD *COSMIC*

Chicanos inherited the word *cosmic* from the Mexican-Latino tradition. Outside the Chicano traditional experience the word *universal* is important. But within the Chicano tradition *cosmic is* traditional. It is synonymous with universal. It is not uncommon to use the term *cosmic-universal* to refer to something of completely inclusive nature, something that excludes no one. Often the worldview of the colonizer and oppressor does not include the oppressed and the colonized. I use the word *cosmic* to include the worldview of the oppressed and colonized.

Among the Latino intellectuals who have written about *La Raza*, José Vasconcelos stands out as unique. Vasconcelos, a Mexican, is the author of *La Raza Cósmica*. After the Mexican Revolution, Vasconcelos was appointed Minister of Education, and his educational innovations were prophetic and revolutionary. He made public education available to the masses of poor in Mexico. In chapter 5, I will speak more about Vasconcelos. At this point I simply point out that the word *cosmic*,[2] as understood within the Chicano tradition, is best described in Vasconcelos's monograph. His vision is explained in this paragraph:

> In Latin America nature will not repeat its partial practices; there will not be a race of only one color, of particular characteristics, which at this one time comes out of forgotten Atlantis. Neither will it be the future nor the fifth, or the sixth race, destined to predominate over its ancestors. What is

going to come out of there is the definitive race, the synthesis race or integral race, made with the genius and with the blood of all peoples, and at the same time more capable of true brotherhood and of a vision truly universal.[3]

This "definitive," "synthesis," "integral" race will fill the planet with the triumphs of the first culture to be truly universal, truly cosmic.[4] In this study I will use the word *cosmic* in this Chicano traditional sense. It is symbolic of our identity as Chicanos.

THE COLONIZED STATUS OF CHICANOS: A COSMIC PHENOMENON

Besides their common racial bonds with Africans,[5] Asians, and indigenous Americans, Chicanos also share common political, economic, social, and spiritual bonds. The colonized status of Chicanos gives them a cosmic identity with other colonized societies in Latin America, Asia, and Africa. We struggle for liberation just as they struggle for liberation. They also know that the exploitation of individual persons comes from a situation of injustice that can be called institutionalized violence.[6] This violence occurs when, because of the structural deficiency of industry and agriculture, of the national and international economy, of cultural and political life, "whole towns lack necessities, live in such dependence as hinders all initiative and responsibility as well as every possibility for cultural promotion and participation in social and political life." Thus fundamental rights are violated.[7] This violence is germane to the Chicano experience in the Southwest.

Rodolfo Acuña wrote in his *Occupied America*:

As my research progressed, I became convinced that the experience of Chicanos in the United States parallels that of the other Third World peoples who have suffered under the colonialism of technologically superior nations.[8]

Further on he states:

I feel that the parallels between the Chicanos' experience in the United States and the colonization of other Third World peoples are too similar to dismiss. Attendant to the definition of colonization are the following conditions:

1. The land of one people is invaded by people from another country, who later use military force to gain and maintain control.

2. The original inhabitants become subjects of the conquerors involuntarily.

3. The conquered have an alien culture and government imposed on them.

4. The conquered become the victims of racism and cultural genocide and are relegated to a submerged status.

5. The conquered are rendered politically and economically powerless.

6. The conquerors feel they have a "mission" in occupying the areas in question and believe that they have undeniable privileges by virtue of their conquest.[9]

To illustrate Acuña's point that Chicanos share an affinity with the impoverished world because of their political colonization I will analyze the first of his six points with examples drawn from the state of Texas: "The land of one people is invaded by people from another country, who later use military force to gain and maintain control."

In the expansionism of the mid-1800s, the United States was not satisfied with the purchase of the Louisiana Territory (from France), nor with the acquisition of the Floridas (from Spain). The United States viewed the Southwest with ambition, for the Southwest was a vast expanse of land with many natural resources.

At the time of the gringo conquest, Mexico was in no position to stop the impulse of Manifest Destiny from taking its territory. Mexico was still trying to pay the war debts it had incurred during its struggle for independence and its war with the Texans. Internally things were not going politically well for the young independent nation either.

In the midst of these crises, General Winfield Scott sailed to Vera Cruz, and General Zachary Taylor marched into Mexico from the north. General Scott took the capital with little resistance. The volunteers from Texas who joined General Taylor blazed a trail of debauchery, rape, and destruction that will never be forgotten by

Chicanos and Mexicans as long as the word honor means anything in this hemisphere. The invasion was so brutally devastating to the Mexicans that even Catholic Anglos joined the Mexican side.[10] Acuña wrote:

> Memoirs, diaries, and news articles written by Anglo Americans document the reign of terror. Samuel F. Chamberlain's *My Confessions* is a record of Anglo racism and destruction. He was only 17 when he enlisted in the Army to fight the "greasers."[11]

Further on Acuña mentions that

> Chamberlain blamed General Taylor not only for collecting over $1 million [from the people by force of arms], but also for letting "loose on the country packs of human bloodhounds called Texas Rangers."[12]

These wanton acts of cruelty by the invading army of regulars and volunteers from the north under General Taylor gave rise to what happened in the Southwest afterwards between Chicanos and gringos.

Even now, military occupation continues in almost every major Chicano city in the Southwest. San Antonio, San Diego, Santa Fe, Corpus Christi, Laredo, Albuquerque, Amarillo, and Austin each have at least one United States military installation; some cities of the Southwest have as many as four or five military bases. Chicanos see this continuing military presence as an overt extension of the conquest. Moreover, in these cities Chicano women continue to be sexually exploited by gringo soldiers. The words of Montesinos and Las Casas resonate from the past.

> These [Mexicans] are they not men? Have they not rational souls? All the wars called conquests were and are most unjust and truly tyrannical.
>
> The natives [Mexicans] in any or all the regions we have invaded in the Indies [Mexico] have acquired the right to make just war upon us and erase us from the face of the earth, and this right will last until the Day of Judgement.[13]

The Texas Rangers are an occupying state police force. To the state they are a symbol of law and order, historical valor, courageous service; they are a distinguished law enforcement force who hold a special place in the history of Texas. To Chicanos, their victims, they symbolize the most repressive and brutal police force in the history of the Southwest. Texas Rangers are a constant reminder of the wanton cruelty that gringos are capable of exerting against *mestizos*. Even today elder Chicanos in Texas still shiver with fear and anger when *los rinches* are mentioned.

Finally, the brutal deaths of young Chicanos (Rodrigues, aged twelve in Dallas, Morales, aged twenty-seven in San Antonio, and Campos Torres, aged twenty-three in Houston), within the last ten years at the hands of police leave no doubt that the invasion is far from over.[14] The invasion is now more subtle. Instead of a strong economic nation forcing itself on a weak economic nation to gain one million square miles of land,[15] it seems as if the police are against one Chicano individual at a time, in different cities and at different moments. Moreover, when these cases were tried, in almost every instance the juries and the judges were all white Anglo-Saxons. Such violations of human rights continue the spirit and the reality of the occupation of the Southwest.

Acuña is not the only authority who maintains that Chicanos are a colonized people. Acuña describes physical colonization; Dr. Jack Forbes, of Far West Laboratory for Educational Research and Development (Berkeley, California), speaks of psychological colonization. In testimony before the United States Civil Rights Commission he explained that Chicanos do not have viable political representation in any of the institutions that shape their destiny because of the "conquered population" syndrome. The following excerpt is taken from the United States Civil Rights Commission report:

> The indigenous people of Mexico, who included those in what is now the American Southwest, first experienced the Spanish conquest, followed by the Anglo-American conquest of the Southwest at the end of the Mexican-American War.
>
> To understand the significance of this syndrome, one must

of course get past the romance and mythology of the supposed westward movement of the pioneers and look at the Anglo-American conquest of the Southwest as we might look at the German march eastward against the Poles or as we might look at the Franco-Norman conquest of England, in other words in a purely detached and objective manner. And if we are to do this, we should see the United States conquest of the Southwest as a very real case of aggression and imperialism, that it involved not only the military phase of immediate conquest, but the subsequent establishment of a colonial office to administer Mexican-American people.

Instead there were many institutions that were created to control and administer Mexican-American people and also to enable the dominant population to acquire almost complete control of the soil and other forms of wealth, of the social institutions, cultural institutions and so on. Now the conquest in the colonial period can be further understood if we think about a community such as the city of Los Angeles in California which has had a large Mexican-American population but in which no major institution of any kind is controlled even proportionately to numbers by the Spanish-speaking population. [The concept of conquest] is very often ignored but I can't emphasize it too much because we're beginning to learn the process of a conquest; particularly the tremendous effect upon people's behavior. . . . For example, a conquered population tends to exhibit certain characteristics such as apathy, apparent indifference, passivity, and a lack of motivation in relation to the goals of the dominant society.[16]

This syndrome must be broken. As a consequence of this syndrome, many Chicanos, young and old, are not aware of their own worth. The problems of alcohol and drugs, the problem of materialism, the problem of belief in the media instead of in the self and the family continue. Liberation concerns itself with the syndrome Dr. Forbes addresses and with the human problems generated from this psychological condition.

Together with the physical and psychological colonization, there exists a spiritual colonization as well. The Catholic Church contributed to the colonization process by ousting the native Mexican clergy and replacing it with a gringo one. After the Texas conflict of 1836 two French bishops were appointed to Texas before the signing of the Treaty of Guadalupe-Hidalgo. After the signing of the treaty, a French bishop was appointed to New Mexico, and a Spanish bishop to California. Arizona's and Colorado's first bishops were also French. Santa Fe's first five archbishops were French. In addition, most members of the religious orders of priests and nuns in the Southwest were French. The Catholic faithful of the Southwest were Chicano, but their spiritual leadership was French or Spanish. This trend continued into the twentieth century when Irish- and German-American bishops replaced the French and Spanish.[17] Although 75 percent of the Catholic population of the Southwest was Chicano, Chicano bishops were not consecrated until the early 1970s.

The systematic denial of spiritual leadership to Chicanos constitutes a form of spiritual colonization. The leaders of the institutional church insured the occupation of the Southwest by denying Chicanos responsible representative leadership in our own Catholic Church. Just as we are treated as strangers in our land, so we are also treated as strangers in our own church, which has existed in the Southwest since the 1500s.

THE RACE-CLASS PERSPECTIVE

Chicanos are darker-skinned than Europeans and consequently, within a colonial system, are considered to be of a lower class economically, socially, and politically. Acuña quotes Manuel Crescíón Rejon, a Mexican diplomat, who prophesied at the signing of the Treaty of Guadalupe-Hidalgo:

> Our race, our unfortunate people, will have to wander in search of hospitality in a strange land, only to be ejected later. Descendants of the Indians that we are, the North Americans hate us, their spokesmen depreciate us, even if they recognize the justice of our cause, and they consider us unworthy to form with them one nation and one society, they clearly

manifest that their future expansion begins with the territory
that they take from us and pushing aside our citizens who
inhabit the land.[18]

Acuña contrasts this statement with one by a gringo historian
writing in 1931 about the mixture of races in the Southwest. This
gringo, Walter Prescott Webb, was once president of the American
Historical Society. He wrote in 1931:

> A homogeneous European society adaptable to new condi-
> tions was necessary. This Spain did not have to offer in
> Arizona, New Mexico and Texas. Its frontier, as it advanced,
> depended more and more on an Indian population. . . . This
> mixture of races meant in time that common soldiers in the
> Spanish service came largely from Pueblo and sedentary
> Indian stock, whose blood when compared to that of the
> Plains Indians, was as ditch water. It took more than a little
> mixture of Spanish blood and mantle of Spanish service to
> make valiant soldiers of the timid Pueblo Indians.[19]

Webb mentions common soldiers. All soldiers are common people.
The officers, however, come from the upper class. They get the
glory, if the common soldier wins. If the common soldier loses, the
officers do not get anything; they lose the war.

I have difficulty with the word "valiant" in reference to a soldier,
especially when the fighting involves a stronger nation against a
weaker nation. We have a word in Spanish for such a strong nation:
aprovechado. The closest phrase in English, though it is not vivid
enough, is "unscrupulous bully." In other words, this person or
nation has the upper hand and attacks the weaker person or nation.
With technology in their favor, how can the notion of "valiant"
even be entertained? Chicanos believe that the only true valiant
soldier is he or she who fights to defend the poor and oppressed.
Soldiers who fight to defend the rich and powerful unknowingly
fight against themselves.

Webb uses the word "timid" incorrectly. The appropriate word is
"afraid," not "timid." One would be afraid of another who has the
power and reputation of a successful and unscrupulous conqueror.
It is not a question of timidness, as if retaliation against injustices

were not desired. It is a question of survival. "Terrified" is an appropriate word. How should one deal with Europeans who break treaties made under oath, who are never satisfied with just a little land, who preach Christian peace with swords at their sides and guns in their hands, and whose only rule in war is to win regardless of method? All this gives rise not to timidity, but to terror. The oppressed are forever afraid and terrorized by the oppressor. There is a profound economy of reason for fear that comes directly from an experience of oppression. Why does the name "Texas Ranger" still strike fear and hate in the hearts of the Chicanos in the Southwest?

THE LANGUAGE PERSPECTIVE

Besides being of a different color and class, Chicanos also speak a different language. The Treaty of Guadalupe-Hidalgo guaranteed us protection of our religion, of our property, and of our civil rights, but it did not mention specifically the protection of our Spanish language, even though that should be included in our human rights. Both Catholic and Protestant churches played a major role in the survival of the language. The Protestant churches trained a Chicano Protestant clergy who spoke both English and Spanish. The Catholic Church, in spite of having a foreign or gringo clergy, also trained its clergy to speak Spanish. So the secular forces suppressed the Spanish language while the religious forces nurtured it. It was difficult for Chicanos to worship in the English tongue of their conquerors.

The constant flow of Mexicans and Southwestern Chicanos back and forth across a political border strengthened the Spanish language among Chicanos. Marriages between Chicanos and Mexicans also insured the survival of the language. Meanwhile, the secular forces made every possible effort to obliterate it.

In most states, the schools were actually mandated by law to make English the language of instruction. An appropriate comment on this type of law was forthcoming recently from Charles Olstad, Assistant Professor of Romance Languages at the University of Arizona: "I had always thought such a law archaic, a carry-over from early days of benighted ethnocentrism, a distorted form of super-patriotism which saw anything non-English as a threat to the nation."[20]

If Chicano students spoke Spanish in the classroom or on the playground, corporal punishment was not out of the question.[21] Many Chicanos who attended public and Catholic schools can vouch for this. But the greater harm to the Chicano child, and consequently to the Chicano population, is described in the following quotation:

> The harm done the Mexican-American child linguistically is paralleled, perhaps even exceeded, by the harm done to him as a person. In telling him that he must not speak his native language, we are saying to him by implication that Spanish and the culture which it represents are of no worth. Therefore (it follows) the people who speak Spanish are of no worth. Therefore (it follows again) this particular child is of no worth. It should come as no surprise to us, then, that he develops a negative self-concept—an inferiority complex. If he is no good, how can he succeed? And if he can't succeed, why try?[22]

THE RELIGIOUS-ECCLESIAL PERSPECTIVE

Although the Catholic Church did help to preserve our Spanish language, it failed to understand our needs and to develop our ecclesiastical leadership. The church managed to alienate itself from the Chicanos. With its foreign intrigue it ignored the Chicano contribution of cosmic-universal awareness. In the Southwest, its concern was to gallicize or Americanize the Chicanos. Chicano religious and secular symbols that are full of meaning for the Chicano were never developed. Our Lady of Guadalupe (chapter 4), Our Lady of San Juan, *La Raza Cósmica* (chapter 5), and *mestizaje* were Chicano symbols that were never developed because Chicanos were kept out of the church hierarchy, out of the priesthood, and out of Catholic academe.

The *Fact Book on Theological Education: 1975–1976* (American Association of Theological Schools) states (p. 9) that only twenty-four Latino students were working toward their master's degree in theology and only thirteen toward their doctorate. In the academic community these thirty-seven theological students represented 18,240,000 Spanish-speaking people in the United States—not even one doctoral candidate per one million people.[23] What does this mean? It means that our representative power in academic theological circles is almost nil.

In the structure of the Catholic Church in the United States, 60 percent of our bishops have Irish surnames; 30 percent have German surnames; 4 percent, Slavic; 2 percent, French; .08 percent, Spanish; .04 percent, Italian; .04 percent are Black; and 6 percent are other.[24] By 1975, only five bishops with Spanish surnames had been consecrated out of some three hundred American bishops in all.[25] In Texas, six bishops have been consecrated from one city, Houston, in the last fifteen years. Only one bishop has been a Chicano. Yet, Lupe Anguiano's study of the Chicano population in Texas showed that Chicanos are the majority in every diocese in Texas except Dallas, where Chicanos are slightly less than a majority.[26] In the American Southwest Chicanos make up 75 percent of the Catholic population.[27]

What do all these figures and statistics prove? They prove that Latinos, in spite of their great numbers in this country, are treated as if they do not exist. According to Dr. Ricardo Sánchez, one of the Chicano leaders interviewed for this book, we Chicanos are not even dealt with. We are forgotten; we are invisible; we are strangers; we are aliens; we are non-beings; we don't exist. Reies López Tijerina wrote:

From San Augustine, Florida, to San Francisco, California, there are 1,799 towns, villages, and cities with Spanish or Mexican names. These together with the names of rivers and mountains of the Southwest, identify the evidence of our existence and immortalize our heritage.[28]

Therefore, we are not invisible or alien in our own land. But we must confront the gringo oppressor and fight against those criminal acts that deny our identity and our existence. Then we will gain the political and theological recognition that we deserve as human beings.

CONCLUSION

The common experiences or inheritances of Chicanos often are opposites that clash together to form a Chicano cosmic-universal experience. The traditional use of the word *cosmic* in the Chicano community is similar to the general use of the word *universal*. Most Chicanos relate the word to José Vasconcelos's book, *La Raza Cósmica*. Chicanos are a group of people colonized within the United States. The colonization is physical, psychological, and spiritual. The *mestizo* race, the lower class status, and the Spanish language are Chicano phenomena that have been used by the dominant white society to keep us apart and segregated. Now these phenomena are utilized by Chicanos to strengthen our identity and slow down the process of assimilation nurtured by the Catholic Church.

Racially, most Chicanos look native American and are poor. We speak Spanish; the educational curriculum strengthens our inferiority complex. Traditionally, our church has been irresponsible in developing a native clergy and native leadership. Today we are millions of people with no representative voice in church or government. We are beginning to realize our situation of oppression and to look for ways to fight toward liberation.

PART 2

Oral Tradition and the Chicano Cosmic Experience of Oppression

CHAPTER 3

Shared Themes of the Chicano
Cosmic Experience of Oppression

Robert Coles employed the "shared themes" method for interviewing in his research with exploited and marginal persons.[1] Robert Jay Lifton used the same method for interviewing surviving atomic bomb victims of Nagasaki and Hiroshima. I felt that this method would be appropriate because of the shared situation of oppression within the Chicano community. There is a difference between the approach of Robert Coles and Robert Jay Lifton and mine. They are on the outside looking in; I am on the inside looking around. I personally share the experience represented in these themes. I have sometimes borrowed the method used in Teófilo Cabestrero's book *Faith: Conversations with Contemporary Theologians* (Orbis Books, 1980). I hope these two methods will aid the reader in grasping the Chicano oral tradition as they have helped me clarify and understand my own endeavor.

The listening approach used by both Coles and Lifton gives the interviewees an opportunity to speak their mind and to develop their point. Cabestrero's method of questioning helps clarify so as to leave no doubt as to what the Chicano leader means on a certain issue.

PERSONS INTERVIEWED FOR THE STUDY

The Chicano experience of oppression is best brought out, I believe, by Chicano leaders as they express their struggles, fears,

33

and hopes for the Chicano community. Let me introduce the two women and seven men I interviewed for this study.

Lupe Anguiano, president of National Woman's Employment and Education, Inc., has long been active in putting facts and figures together for the benefit of the Chicano community. In a study of the major dioceses in the Southwest, she discovered that almost all of them had a majority of Chicano Catholics.[2] Anguiano resides in San Antonio where she defends women against church and state leaders who tend to undermine woman's role in society and in the Chicano culture. She was an active participant in and supporter of the Declaration of Mexico, which was an outcome of the United Nations International Women's Year Conference in the summer of 1975. All countries except the United States and Israel adopted the plan outlined by the Declaration.[3] She acknowledges the difference between Chicano liberation and Latin American liberation objectives.

Rubén Armendariz, Chicano theologian and educator, directs the Latino Studies Program at McCormick Theological Seminary in Chicago. This was the first Latino theological program to be accredited in the United States. A Presbyterian minister from Galveston, Texas, he moved to Chicago to direct the Latino program. It has been very successful and is a milestone in Latino theological education. His sensitive and careful thinking acknowledges both the Catholic and Protestant contributions of the Chicano community. His program is not exclusively Chicano. It includes ministry to Puerto Ricans, Cubans, Mexicans, and other Latino groups in the United States.

Tomás Atencio is working on his Ph.D. in sociology at the University of New Mexico. He serves as president on the board of directors of Academia, a non-profit organization incorporated in New Mexico for developing and teaching Chicano culture. He has a gift for analyzing the Chicano experience in New Mexico. A member of the Presbyterian Church, he is presently engaged in an intellectual, ecclesiastical, and political battle to save Old Town from the Sun Belt entrepreneurs.

Bishop Gilbert Chávez, auxiliary bishop of San Diego, was one of the fifteen bishops attending a pastoral work conference in Riobamba, Ecuador, that was disrupted by military police. About eighty persons—bishops, priests, nuns, and lay persons—were put into a bus at gunpoint and taken to the San Gregorio police barracks in Quito.[4] Later the government apologized for its mistake, but the bishops had experienced firsthand what common-folk organizers experience under military democratic dictatorships.

When I talked to Chávez over the telephone, he told me that questions on liberation theology could not be discussed. His bishop had asked him to refrain from making statements on the subject. That restraint seemed to compromise the plight of the poor.

Dr. José Ángel Gutiérrez, founder of La Raza Unida Party, endeavored to help the Chicanos by initiating a political party of, by, and for Chicanos. He was politically successful in some southwestern counties of Texas, especially Crystal City, center of much political controversy. Before Gutiérrez, Anglos (15 percent of the population) controlled the political, social, economic, and ecclesiastical order of Crystal City, whereas Chicanos (85 percent of the population) controlled nothing. He now teaches in a remote area of the Pacific Northwest to support himself and his family. No university in the Southwest will give him a job in his field of political science because of his political commitment to Chicano needs and rights.

Dolores Huerta, vice-president of the United Farm Workers, has devoted her life, together with César Chávez, to the fight for justice and dignity for farm workers. Besides being an organizer, she is the mother of twelve children. Seeing her and listening to her speak makes one recall the long years of struggle for the farm workers. She lives in La Paz, Calif., with her husband and children. When I interviewed her in her home she was busy amidst a certain peace and joy.

Msgr. Longinus Reyes is chancellor of the diocese of Austin, Texas, one of the oldest *colonias* of Chicanos in that state. Austin is the seat of the University of Texas system. Reyes was born in Lockhart, twenty miles outside Austin, to a migrant farm-worker family. He is one of eleven children, four of whom chose a religious vocation.

Reyes is one of the three persons responsible for the progressive theological and pastoral developments in his diocese. A clear and wise thinker, he has uncommon theological-political visions for

Chicanos. Being in a powerful position has not changed the priest's commitment to his people. I found him with young people, with whom he has a charisma. They look up to him; they respect him. He is their friend. Because his days are busy, I interviewed him between one and four o'clock in the morning. He was angry with the ecclesiastical, political, and media powers, who were more concerned with their own interests than with human-rights violations in society. Reyes is one of the few individuals I know who tries to understand both the Anglo mind and the Chicano mind for the sake of a more humane society. It is not an easy task when one remembers the history of Chicano and Anglo-Saxon relations in the Southwest. The history has been a brutal and bloody one for Chicanos.

Dr. Ricardo Sánchez, Chicano poet, is the only Chicano leader I interviewed who has written extensively. He has published nine books of poetry. Sánchez is also the only one I interviewed who can speak from the side of those who have been imprisoned. Prison has been the fate of many Chicanos in the barrio. It has been the fate of many of the oppressed, especially if they challenge the powers that be.

His thinking is broad. His insights and visions leave many of us far behind. If I were to specify his focus, I would have to say it is humanity. Whatever hurts, limits, or impedes humanity is suspect to him. He questions everything. Because of this his discoveries are enlightened. He feels that if he compromises his visions, he will limit his human potential. In the tradition of those who fight for liberation, Sánchez takes sides with the oppressed.

Reies López Tijerina, an evangelical Pentecostal minister, has taken the bull by the horns. The bull in this case is the federal government. Tijerina and his followers in *La Alianza Federal de Pueblos Libres* possess land grants which state that they are the legal and rightful owners of large sections of the Santa Fe National Forest and other sections of the Southwest. For three hundred years the New Mexicans farmed, tilled, and grazed their sheep, goats, and cattle on land given to them by the king of Spain under the auspices of the Roman Catholic Church. After 1848, the New Mexicans gradually lost all control and possession of their (native) lands in New Mexico.

For Tijerina, the struggle for land is not only a political quest; it is also a spiritual mission for justice against the oppression of

Chicanos in the Southwest by the United States government. Just because a country is powerful and can manifest its destiny does not give it the right to break international law, which upholds treaties made between two sovereign nations. When the United States broke the Treaty of Guadalupe-Hidalgo, which guaranteed property rights, religious liberty, and protection of rights to Mexican citizens, it broke international law. The United States has become accustomed to breaking treaties, as it continues to do with the native Americans. It thought it could do the same with Mexicans until Tijerina came on the scene. His resistance makes him one of the strongest moral and legal leaders for Chicanos in the Southwest. Many Chicanos have not recognized this yet. To no one's surprise, Tijerina has served three years of a twenty-year sentence in federal prison. He and other Pueblo de San Joaquín families are living on a section of the 1,000,000 acres of land the U.S. federal government has silently turned over to them because of the land grant dispute. Tijerina does not compromise his struggle for Chicanos and the oppressed.

Recently, as a result of his research into the land grant issue, Tijerina has claimed that Hispanos in the New World are descendants of the Israelites. He claims that just as our land was stolen illegally so has our Israelite name been stolen.

All of these men and women are leaders because of their dedication, their commitment, their insight, their experience, their prophecy, and their love for our Chicano community. Full of hope, they fight and struggle against tremendous odds. Their fight for justice has been long and tedious, but they hang on. They don't quit. There are others, but I chose these nine because of their involvement in the Chicano movement during the late sixties and early seventies and because of their availability.

With most of the leaders I interviewed I spent the better part of a day. I had a chance to experience their milieu by visiting them in their own location. I ate with them. I shared their feelings, fears, struggles, and hopes. None was rich; two were poor, three were lower middle class, and four were middle class. All were struggling. Six were employed, two were unemployed, and one was about to lose his job. All were generous with their time and energy. Their *casa* was my *casa*.[5] All showed a common joy and peace with life and a happiness that comes from a sense of purpose.

SHARED THEMES

The themes through which I chose to investigate our oral tradition are these:

1. *Machismo y La Mujer*
2. Racism-Classism
3. Education and Labor
4. Violence and Nonviolence
5. *El respeto al derecho ajeno es la paz*, "Respect for the rights of others is peace" (Benito Juárez)
6. The Land
7. Fatalistic and Anarchistic Tendencies
8. The Catholic Church
9. Theology
10. The Symbol of Exodus
11. The Religious-Spiritual Symbol of Guadalupe (chapter 4)
12. The Secular-Spiritual Symbol of *La Raza Cósmica* (chapter 5)

The first seven themes emphasize social, economic, political, and psychological issues. Of the seven, the first four are common to all peoples. The next three are particular to the Chicano experience. These are unique to our experience because of the way Chicano life revolves around these issues: Many Chicanos quote Benito Juárez; most are familiar with the conquest of the land; and fatalism and anarchistic tendencies may have positive rather than negative meaning in the culture.

The last five themes emphasize religious or spiritual issues. Three of these fit a different kind of religious category; they are symbols around which we can organize our experiences of oppression and our hope for liberation.

I selected these twelve themes because of their importance to the Chicano community. I judged them to be important because of my own personal experience as a Chicano and because of questions raised as I studied articles and books written about and by Chicanos. These themes deal with Chicano liberation. One cannot speak about liberation without mentioning these social, political, economic, psychological, and religious issues, nor without mentioning these symbols.

Other themes and symbols could have been selected, but these twelve are the most pertinent to this study, because they deal with questions of Chicano cultural survival. Directly or indirectly, these issues have been continuing major factors in our situation of oppression. Symbols such as Guadalupe and *La Raza* have been misused in the past to oppress us; they have also been used to liberate us. The symbol of the Exodus has recently been used in Latin American and Black liberation theologies. Interestingly enough, this fundamental theme of liberation theology does not politically fit the Chicano situation of oppression in the Southwest, as I will show from the responses on this issue.

All nine leaders interviewed responded to each shared theme. Instead of giving here nine edited responses for each theme, I selected those few which in my estimation gave a more comprehensive vision of Chicano experience. At times I will leave idiomatic expressions in Spanish in order to emphasize the tone, color, and meaning of the responses.

The untaped conversations I had with the Chicano leaders were as valuable as those recorded on the tapes. Perhaps they were more valuable because the information in them was not monitored by academic pursuit. It was communication that came from the heart and spirit on the spur of the moment. I asked myself: Why should these committed individuals trust me with their information, thought, and ideas? I felt that because of their writings and contributions they were not strangers to me. By reading about their spiritual, social, and political dedication to the Chicano community and to humanity I knew something about them. Yet they knew little or nothing about me except what they learned through the themes that I shared with them. Nevertheless they confided in me and told me information that I cannot even repeat for fear that it would hurt them, their families, and their endeavors for justice. In total, the material they shared is for me a treasure house of theological, social, and political cosmic awareness. For this I thank them and hold their trust dearly.

Machismo y la Mujer

I proposed the following shared theme to the nine Chicano leaders:

Leo D. Nieto, in his article "The Chicano Movement and the Churches in the United States," beckons us to deal with the issue of the oppression of Chicano women by Chicano men: "If the matter of equality between the sexes is not resolved, then true liberation cannot be achieved by Chicanos. If all of us are not free, then none of us are free." What steps can we take against the machismo *concept, which dehumanizes women in our society?*

DOLORES HUERTA: The church has been responsible for a lot of the *machismo* because it does not do anything to counteract it. I think that it is important that the church take a role and make a moral statement, which it has not done. The church really contributes to the oppression of women. It's a male-dominated church. The churches are all male dominated, and the roles they have for women are all male-dominated roles, in spite of the Virgin of Guadalupe. . . . I am just saying that the church has not done anything at all that I can see. Even in the whole idea of children—which I think is very important—the church has done nothing in terms of helping women with those children. The Catholic Church should be number one in terms of setting up educational facilities for children and they should be helping Latino women who have such tremendous cultural problems in this country with their kids. Yet the church is doing very little.

•

LUPE ANGUIANO: I have had so many experiences with the whole *macho, machismo* situation. It is strong, and it is a reality. I believe that in our struggle for liberation I have seen a lot of bright Chicanas just being isolated from the total decision-making process of Chicano organizations. Perhaps they didn't agree with some of the things Chicanos were doing. My experience, particularly my latest experience, with the church is how you are looked upon. If you have different ideas, and different points of view, there is just no way that you can really open a channel of communication to expound and be respected on your ideas. I think that different ideas and different points of view are always seen as a threat. Number one, if you're not supporting; number two, if you're not a sister, a mother, or a wife, then your ideas become suspicious because you become like a power base that the Chicano has to deal with.

I believe that we are not going to have liberation until we start respecting the other 50 percent of our population. I see more and more Chicanas who in order to survive will just have to fight back. You find very few Chicanos or Chicano organizations that really want to talk about the issue of welfare. I have not seen Chicano, Mexican-American organizations who really come to grips with priorities of the Mexicana. It's always: we have to liberate the men first and then we will take care of you later. If you try to do the other, it's interpreted as disloyalty. The biggest thing they use on you is that you're in a white woman's lib kick.

GUERRERO: We always hear the criticism you mentioned, that the Chicana is just following in the footsteps of the Anglo-Saxon, who is in a whole different social stratum. As a consequence the issue that Leo is trying to bring out is not even dealt with.

ANGUIANO: My big argument with a lot of Chicanos is that they only use that as an excuse so as not to deal with the priority issues that we want to deal with. But the classic thing that happens to us is that when we go to deal with the Anglo woman's liberation movement, they bring this to us, "Well, are you a feminist first or a Chicana?" Then you go to the Chicanos, and they ask, "Are you a Chicana first or a feminist?" Then you know you're in a bind with both groups. Both want you to join them first and you know I'm not a half Chicana woman. It's not a question of either-or. The Chicano male has no right to question the Chicana's integrity.

GUERRERO: In other words that question is not really the issue. The real issue is the reality that exists in the relationship of women and men within the same culture. In addition to the political, the economic, and the social, there is a spiritual dimension that we need to deal with. I think Leo and you are both hinting at that. There is a barrier that we males possess traditionally and culturally.

ANGUIANO: It's socialization. I see that every day in working with women on welfare, trying to help them get into a job and get control of their lives. A great deal of the problem is the way the woman sees herself. Also, we are victims of socialization in that we ourselves see the men as being "the head of us." I don't think that it's really the problem of the men. I don't hold men responsible for many socialization problems that have to do with a woman's liberation. Some of it is the men's fault, but most isn't because a great deal has to do with the way a woman sees herself, what she wants to do with her own liberation.

I think that the second and third generations are going to be able to handle this problem better than I am handling it. Right now some women blame the male for all their problems. I don't agree with that. I feel that a lot of it is a problem of socialization. Yes, we are going to have to deal politically with the male, and I have a hard time dealing with the Chicano. In a sense, I think that what I'm doing right now in my work is allowing myself to express myself by making decisions on my own, irrespective of males that I have worked for in the past.

I guess I would answer the problem of male-female relationships as follows: number one, the problem of socialization and the idea we as women are brought up with, that man is the head of the family with a subservient wife. The other is that the whole social and political structure is built to favor the man as the head of the family. You see that in welfare; you see that in divorce. The man is always supposed to take care of the woman. We have that written into our laws; the woman is supposed to be dependent.

GUERRERO: In the Catholic Church?

ANGUIANO: The Catholic Church is the worst as far as equality of women is concerned.

GUERRERO: But why is it that we put our Blessed Mother on a pedestal, yet we treat our wife, our sisters, and our daughters unequally?

ANGUIANO: I think that is such a paternalistic, oppressive thing. Ultimately, what I see in that protective sort of hypocrisy is the excuse to oppress the woman. I have been invited to speak to a lot of Chicano gatherings. When I'm scheduled to be the speaker in a male and female audience about the liberation of the Mexicana or Mexican-American woman, immediately you find the male putting his arm around "his woman," cuddling her very close and almost being protective of what it is that I am about to say. So as to say, "Hey, I'm not that way. I always throw out the garbage, I love my wife. I do this and I do that." In other words, the male—and perhaps it's partly our fault because the *mujer* has raised the man to do that—believes that liberation is really cuddling, being protective, and loving the woman.

GUERRERO: That is tradition.

ANGUIANO: Tradition, yet when you interpret that and talk about the woman building an economic base so that she can take care of herself financially, you are accused of destroying the culture. When you talk about the real physical survival which is the economic, then "you are threatening my *machismo*." The issue is the development of the talent, the skills, the career of the woman. It is so hard to deal with Chicanos, with Hispanic men, on this question because they interpret the fact that they love and protect their woman as being a liberation, a cultural phenomenon. They want to cling to this. They think that anything that will change this pattern is going against our culture. I am vehemently against that because it is really an excuse men use to keep the woman barefoot, pregnant, and economically subservient to them.

GUERRERO: I want to add a little dimension to that. Oppression causes something within the mind of the oppressed, especially the male. Within the culture there is a lot of emphasis on *machismo*. Yet it's a thwarted kind of *machismo* because the oppression makes the man dependent or makes him want to be dependent upon someone else, usually his wife. In our culture there exists an element of insecurity. Perhaps this insecurity leads a man to need someone dependent upon him, his spouse, but at the same time he is enslaving her.

ANGUIANO: On the one hand you have the people that are oppressed. They perhaps become the victims by promulgating their own oppression because of how they feel about themselves. Then on the other hand, having been put through that oppression, the male acts as the oppressor against women. The strong women that stand up are ostracized.

Another example is getting Chicanos into good political positions. You struggle and fight to get some Chicanos in and you discover that the situation remains the same. The other day I went before the CETA. All of the decision makers are Chicanos. I went to argue for a welfare reform project. You know what? While I was arguing with them a flash came through my mind, and I saw them as white men. I said to myself, "What a fool. You fought for your people when you were on the picket line and in the struggle, and here all you have really done is just substitute a brown face for a white face. It was easier for me to deal with that white face than for me to deal with that brown face as a *mujer*. It is awful. It is so hard to go back and deal with that brown face. Now I have to fight the Chicanos so that the issues of the Chicana can be dealt with.

GUERRERO: Right, and it's going to be a more difficult fight.

ANGUIANO: The Chicanos will go and support a *gringa* because that *gringa* isn't a threat to their power base. It's pretty sad; we've got to destroy that. That's not a cultural value. The *mujer* is strong. I think part of the reason is that the *mujer* has had to shoulder a heck of a lot of oppression, and so she has become a strong force in our community. She has moved forward for one reason: in order to survive. The very oppressive situation forces you to be strong. I often wonder what would have happened if the woman had been on an equal base with the man, economically, spiritually, and so on—what she would do.

•

MSGR. LONGINUS REYES: This one is a real tough one. I think when we talk about racism, about the gringo, or about the system or whatever you want to talk about, then you can rally people against it. But when you talk about Chicano men, then we've got problems. I'm saying this generically. How do we really deal with this question of equality between Chicano women and men?

First of all we have to be aware of this *machismo* in the bad sense. We can't just say it's something that's there or something that others do as men, even as women. I would think it's even more with women than with men because I think the one that has the greatest influence on little boys growing up is the female. She's the one who's determining how he is going to think and how he is going to relate to his sister or sisters. That's why I'm saying that I think first of all we have to come to grips with this whole concept of *machismo*. Chicano men are going to have to deal with it and become aware that it's there. But I think Chicanas are going to have to be more conscious of it. They are going to have to be aware of how they are making *machos*. I see this constantly. Yet I see other instances where the mother is really making her son conscious that his sister is equal to him; that he can't just run over her because he's male, and that he needs to be sensitive and aware of her, of his sister, as a full person with full rights and responsibilities just as he has.

But I look around in our society in our barrios and, hell, it is the guys who are out late at night, but no way is that girl going to be out late at night. And who's enforcing that? Many times, it's the mother. Who's the one that has to do all the household chores? The female, the young Chicana, but not her brother. He doesn't have to do that. Who waits on him? Mom to a large extent is the one responsible for making the daughters wait on her son. That needs to be changed, it has to be changed.

I see in our families that it's the mother who takes charge of the family many times. The father goes to work and comes home. He can sit down and have his beer, have his supper, holler at the kids. They have to do what he says. But what kind of image is that projecting to the sons and to the daughters? As they see the relationship between their father and their mother, it's the mom that has to stay at home. It's the mom that has to go to work just like the father does, but yet when she gets home, mom is the one who has to do all the work. Dad can sit down, have a beer, and watch T.V. These things need to be changed. The problem is compounded by the whole attitude of the dominant society. But it just seems to me that we as Chicano men have to be aware of this.

I think that we in the church have to give an equal role to the woman because symbols are very important. If all we see are males on the altar, in whatever capacity, then we are already saying something. If it weren't for the women, the Chicanas around here, we couldn't run this parish, we couldn't run the churches. Our whole experience in Latin America has been that the ones that are running the churches are the women, *las mujeres*. It's just something that we blind ourselves to. We don't recognize what is always there. But the church is already run to a large extent by the Latinas; it's theirs. So I think that in the home, in the church, and in other institutions—but generally in the first two because they do impact tremendously on attitudes and on families—there is a need to be very conscious of the *machismo* element.

Racism-Classism

The shared theme was stated as follows:

Our people use the term "todos hijos de Dios o todos hijos del diablo (all children of God or all children of the devil)."[6] *How would this statement relate to the issue of racism or classism? Latin American, European, and Anglo-Saxon theology have said that the real issue is class. Black liberation theology has contended that the issue is one of race. Judging from our own experience, what will Chicanos say?*

MSGR. LONGINUS REYES: I'm not going to say that the issue is one of class. There's no way. I had a friend of mine when I was first ordained in my first assignment who worked for the police department. We argued because I used to say that we got discriminated against because we were Chicanos. He firmly believed that if you try hard enough you can make it. He had a daughter in the Catholic high school there where I was first assigned and she graduated at the top of the class. She went along with her Anglo friends to apply for a position at the telephone company. Everything was going along fine with her application until they found out her last name was Rodríguez. And in this red-neck town, like we have all over Texas, she didn't get the job. It was obvious that the only reason was because her name was Rodríguez. I mean she wasn't dark-skinned, she was light, and that's why they didn't detect it until right at the end. Not only that, but her two Anglo friends knew what the real reason was. They were very upset because they had copied from her all through high school. That's how her two friends had graduated. They knew she was smarter than they were. Her father called me later and told me, "It's race, it's not economics, it's not education, it's not class, it's race." The thing about it is that Chicanos here in the barrio will criticize just like Captain Rodríguez until they experience it. Until they go through it, they say it's not race. But in the meantime they're just contented.

If we want to look at a situation in a community, look at busing and segregation. That's obviously race. It has nothing to do with class. You know the whole housing pattern is already set up by racists. Look at any city in this country. You know where the Black lives, you know where the Chicano lives or the Chinese or the Vietnamese. You know where they live and you know where the Anglo lives. It's all defined. Yet they try to say that this whole desegregation, this whole business has nothing to do with race. We have to recognize it for what it is. It is race pure and simple.

•

LUPE ANGUIANO: I definitely think it's a matter of class. I don't think that the color of our skin has really been a major factor. However, a Chicano with money can integrate more into society than a Black person who has money. There have been a lot of studies, one by Dr. Cecilia Juárez, who believes that the class-color issue is valid. The whole basis of her research is that color is a major factor of discrimination. Another person who did research in that area is Dr. Amado Padilla. He is a psychologist and is director of the research center for Spanish-speaking at UCLA. I believe he has some pretty strong arguments that color is a factor in discrimination.

•

RICARDO SÁNCHEZ: It is both, racism and classism. But it's more than that; it's even deeper than that. There are acts of racism and classism. That's not deniable. Racists hate others; actually, they hate themselves more than they hate others. In their own limitations, they need to find somebody inferior to them. But the problem is with the person, not the object who is being hated. Of course the object that is being hated or actually the subject that is being hated is being undermined, hindered and hurt, and sometimes destroyed by the racism of another. I don't deny that. But also in a very real sense, having gone through all this personally, I learned that I couldn't hate. I'm not saying I learned to love them or respect them. But to hate them would demean me. It would make them important and me unimportant. I feel that nobody is worthy of hate. People that hate usually feel very limited, very meaningless, regardless of their social position. There is such an underlying self-denigration within them that they must hate others to make themselves important.

Racism, which initially emanated from that individual lack of self, has become institutionalized. Unfortunately, it is very easy to institutionalize. Not only do we now have the problem of individual race against other individuals, but we have a collectivity of races against other collectivities. This is abetted by the institutions that exist, which of course make sure that certain people don't have a voice.

The United States is the fourth or fifth largest Spanish-speaking country in the world. But this is not reflected in the mass media, because we don't exist. We have a few tokens here and there but we don't have any programs geared toward us. We are a nation within a nation. Yet we don't truly exist. We're consumers and everything, but we're not even dealt with as consumers. Most of us Chicanos are of the lower class in terms of economic power, political reality, and social status, but we are human. Socially we are a lower-class people because of our lack of resources and our lack of mobility. We don't have any of that; we have stagnation societally. That is classism definitely. We suffer from all these ills. We're even treated worse than Blacks because Blacks at least get looked at and dealt with. We're not even looked at or dealt with in any way. Even though your reality may be discussed while you are there, still they don't acknowledge you.

GUERRERO: You said that we are oppressed in a different way—is this one of the ways?

SÁNCHEZ: Yes, because the Black person is acknowledged. The American Indian isn't acknowledged either. They have some fantasy that neuters Indians. They're on a mantlepiece. They're a piece of turquoise. They're a feather. They don't exist. They're exotic creatures, whatever that means. People deal with them that way, or otherwise they are conquered Indians. It's a weird phenomenon; we see it in our culture in terms of women. We are always trying to keep our women pure. The same thing with the Indians, we want to keep them pure and stoic. But the Indians are not stoics.

GUERRERO: You said that we're oppressed differently. Does it have to do with invisibility?

SÁNCHEZ: Well, remember that Indios and Chicanos have one thing in common: we are not subcultural groups who came here to submerge our personalities and acquire the trappings of the oppressor or whoever was in power. I mean we didn't become German-

Anglo Americans. We stayed Mexicanos, Chicanos, even though some of us want to be Mexican-Anglo American. A lot of us continue with our culture, our idioms, our values, and our family patterns. All those things are important to the vast majority of us. We continue being different and thus respond to the world from a different perspective.

There is a Black language but it is predicated on English. I mean Chicanos have Spanish. We are still *mestizos* in our language. Therefore we think very differently from the Anglo-Saxon. Things have different values for us and different consequences. We look at an object and we see it not through glasses that have been tinted by white America, but from our culture. Blacks call themselves Black—an English word. They don't call themselves Zulus or a derivation of Zulu. They call themselves an English word. Not us, we are Chicanos. Chicanos! A word that is foreign to English-speaking America. Our oppression then comes from our being truly invisible to them because they can't understand us, so they just negate our existence. They can't truly understand the Indio who is truly Indio so they negate the Indio's existence. They create nonsensical fantasies about us so that they don't have to deal with us. They create romantic illusions about us, like Zorro, but they have no basis at all, not even coloration, because Zorro was not *mestizo*.

GUERRERO: If you look at the situations of Chicanos in the professions and at those that have been more or less successful, isn't it true that the lighter you are the more opportunities are available to you as opposed to the more *trigueños*.

SÁNCHEZ: Yes, color definitely does create a barrier to opportunity. Look at our own community, how they respond, "Oh, what a beautiful baby, he's so light." A blond Chicano is born and they're all saying, "Oh, he's so beautiful." As if color is beauty in and of itself.

GUERRERO: And when he's dark?

SÁNCHEZ: Oh, poor baby, he's so dark. But "poor baby" is said more as condolence, because he is going to have to get hurt because of his color. So we have to counteract that, like the Blacks, who tell themselves that Black is beautiful. And we counteract that by realizing that beauty is multicolored, multilingual, the *Raza Cós-mica*. If each human individual could become strong, if each

individual could acquire the kind of anarchism that is very buttress-
ing where the person is self-determined, self-motivated, able inde-
pendently to deal with self and others, then perhaps we wouldn't
have that need to put down other people. We could see the beauty
inherent in every individual and every human being.

Education and Labor

I asked this question from a narrow perspective, as was called to
my attention by the persons I interviewed. The theme was stated as
follows:

*A vicious circle of the culture of nonbeing exists in relation to
these two areas: education and labor. In North American
society you need money to get an education and you need an
education to make money. If you do not have one of the two,
you do not have the other. How do you envision breaking this
vicious circle that dehumanizes us as a group of oppressed
people? Also will you explain how this vicious circle keeps us
in perpetual poverty?*

JOSÉ ÁNGEL GUTIÉRREZ: First of all the educational system
was not built for us. I think it is Dr. José Ángel Cárdenas who
compares the American educational system to a shoe store. Chicano children go to the educational shoe store asking for a size
seven, and the salesperson there tells them that the shoes only come
in size six. So therefore to fit our feet to those shoes they cut off our
toes. That's the analogy he uses to explain the incompatibility of
our needs with the system's services. And because we don't get
prepared, trained, or supported in those fields that we bring to the
school we end up being psychologically atrophied. We learn all the
biases against ourselves; we learn to hate our history. We learn to
hate and denigrate our contribution, and we learn to be rejected by
the system. I don't think we'll ever be able to break out of our
predicament if we adhere to the educational system as it now
stands.

We Chicanos have only one college of higher education and it is
not even accredited. Structurally there's no way for us to ever make
any headway in terms of becoming professionals. Mexico, with its

program *Becas para Atzlán* (Scholarships for Atzlán), is training more Chicano doctors than any one institutional medical school in the United States. Chicanos are having to go to Mexico to be trained as doctors. The grant that the Mexican government gave to the Committee for Rural Democracy of some $12 million is the largest grant ever given by anybody, including foundations, to a Chicano group. Only Project Ser, Department of Labor Contractors, surpasses that amount.

•

MSGR. LONGINUS REYES: I don't know if this circle can be broken unless the whole system is changed. The system itself is experiencing problems because you produce from the educational tool. It's really a question of the way the system is today. Basically it belongs to a very few people; the crumbs come to the rest of the people. And with these crumbs they do the best they can. But the system belongs to the few. To change that you have to take it away from the few and distribute it among the greater portions of the populace. You're really talking about the educational and the economic systems.

But the way it is right now I don't see how you are really going to effect any change within that system because you just can't make it up there without that stamp of approval from those few. The way it is set up only an exceptional kid around here that's got a high academic average will be given the opportunity of a college education. But by and large the average person doesn't stand a chance. And yet the system will always look and say, "See, he or she made it." But the one thing they're not telling you is that this one is the exceptional person. They're never going to tell you that. Then they'll use this exceptional person as a model to all the average Joes and Janes and Marias and Panchitos and say, "See he/she made it. Why can't you make it? It's because you're lazy. It's because you don't have enough initiative and drive."

When I look around here in the barrio and see all the people and kids coming up, I don't want to kid them about getting a good education in high school, because that high-school education isn't worth very much. They don't even know how to read much less be able to pass the SAT or ACT tests. They don't stand a chance.

That's why I'm never going to tell them that. What I am going to do is to tell them to do the best they can and to try to get them to see what's really going on and how it's affecting them.

•

DOLORES HUERTA: I think you break the circle by destroying the myth that you have to have an education to be a human being. The fact that you're born makes you a human being. An education doesn't do anything to make you a better person. Education and intelligence are two different things. Education is a matter of opportunity. Those that go to school often think they're better than others. I'm sure it helps you get a job, but if an education means helping you become part of the establishment or turn against your own people, then what kind of education is that? How many people do we see that get an education and really say: I'm getting an education to help someone else? It looks very good when you see the number of Chicano teachers, the number of Chicano attorneys, but they think of an education as being the end, the goal, instead of the beginning of the work. Education should be the beginning of what you can do, not the end. It's not a resting place.

So I think that one of the big problems we have in the Chicano movement is the whole ideal of education. It's not really being studied or looked at. A philosophy of Chicano education has not been developed. We don't have the kind of education to develop leadership. We, the Chicanos who are being educated in the gringo system, are being educated as conformists and not as leaders. It's very hard for the people once they get out of college to fight the system or to change it. You do not see an educational model being developed to really enhance the mind of the Chicano. It hasn't happened yet.

•

TOMÁS ATENCIO: Education is important. One reason is that it means certification and without that you can't get into the system. I think that that is one of the worst things about education—it sanctions certification. For example, my first profession was social work. As a social worker I could work within a welfare system or an agency. But as a social worker I also had skills enabling me to be a private practitioner or a therapist, but for that I needed certification. Why? Because the therapists that are Ph.D.s in psychology or M.D. psychiatrists control the laws. So my education then has to be increased to fit within the standards of those who are making the laws for me. That is strictly politics. The business of education is certification. The problem is that failure is built in. So one of the major problems is to break in. You can't be a professor, even if you know your business, unless you have been terribly well published or you have a Ph.D. That's certification.

Now what about the education? I think education has several components. One of the components is skills. You need those. The best place to get those skills is in an organized institution, starting with the first grade all the way up. Knowledge is cumulative in institutions. They are the places that harbor and archive that knowledge. Then they have ways of transmitting it. In terms of being effective as a transmitter of knowledge, the educational system leaves a lot to be desired. If Chicanos were able to meet the political problem of certification and the use of cumulative knowledge, then they wouldn't need schools because the methods that the schools have for transmitting knowledge are really bad.

Another component of education is awareness. I think this is where Paulo Freire's contributions are really great. What do I mean by awareness? It is consciousness of who you are as a human being, who you are within the cultural context, who you are in the economic system, who you are in the world. Education doesn't give that awareness. Education gives you a skill and an ideology. It gives you an ideological perspective that will fit you into the dominant society. I think that the churches could be a tremendous vehicle, could play an instrumental role in this whole question of awareness for Chicanos.

•

REIES LÓPEZ TIJERINA: I have ten children; four are still at home. My four have not gone to school for seven years. Why? Because the Anglo terrorized them, put fire bombs in my home. They kidnapped three members of my family and raped two. These crimes were openly published. The criminals were all government officials.

So when it comes to education I am in a position to say blankly: Why was I terrorized and consequently my children deprived of an education? Because of what I believe, what I know, which is very dangerous to the legal system of the Anglo. This means that what the Anglo is teaching is Anglo mentality. You are a victim of the Anglo. You come here to my home, you know nothing about what I am saying. In other words, Andrés, this is Babylon the Great and the Anglo government is educating us to their liking.

But even if we graduate and we become lawyers, we are outside the mainstream. They have many, many ways. Just like they did with me here in New Mexico. They sent me to prison. They kept these facts of my children not going to school from the news media. The news media doesn't publish it! The world doesn't know that I, copatriarch of the Chicano movement, am not allowed to send my kids to school because of terror. Yet, when Andrei Sakharov in Russia is oppressed, the United States makes a special campaign for him. Why doesn't someone make a campaign about my children?

So what kind of education are you talking about? Will you rephrase your question? The problem in speaking about liberation, liberation theology, and exodus is that you can't do it within the legal system. You are a slave, a victim. Just like water and oil don't mix, it's the same thing with our rights and the United States system. I am saying that the question is irrelevant because first, you should speak about our history, our rights, international law, real law, the true history of the United States. Then we should speak on whether we have a right, whether we are given that educational right, and to what extent.

GUERRERO: Are you questioning education?

TIJERINA: This country teaches their children to be oppressors. Would you call that education? Real education? That is the trouble with the illegal Anglo system. Very soon it is going to discover that it is weak in the law. They have built their political and legal systems on sand.

•

LUPE ANGUIANO: I believe the Blacks have survived because they have had separate educational institutions where they have learned engineering, law, medicine, and so on. We haven't been able to make it in the educational institutions because they don't speak our language and they do not relate to our culture. All they do is tell us that we are no good, dumb, mentally retarded. It's very interesting when you look at the history of Texas right after the so-called Independence of Texas—one of the first things was to strike at our Spanish. I believe the exclusion that the educational system practices is really where we are first dehumanized.

For example, when I was in Washington working in bilingual education, we did some studies of Chicano kids and Indian kids. The Indian kids were from the Navajo reservation. The Chicanitos were from Melabar School in Los Angeles. Dr. Valopalomas, president of the Human Development Institute in San Diego, translated the Stanford-Binet test into Spanish and gave it to Chicanitos. He gave it to them in English and Spanish. The little kids had no formal education in Spanish. Yet they scored far better in those tests in Spanish than they did in English. Those tests were given to the kids as they progressed through the first and second grade. By the time they reached the second grade they were on the borderline of mental retardation. The Indian kids taking the Peabody Test in their language scored of average intelligence. When they got to the second grade the same test was given to them in their language and in English. They bordered on mental retardation. The process of education was a process of mental retardation.

It's how the teacher looks at you and the way the teacher identifies with you. If kids speak Spanish, they are looked down upon. That has a lot to do with your self-concept. When your self-concept is destroyed, your learning processes are blocked. Thus, you're not able to grow and develop intellectually. I think that Blacks survived because it was Blacks teaching Blacks. Bilingual education was supposed to solve this, but it didn't. And the reason is that bilingual education was used not as an education for the whole school but rather to label the Chicanito. Bilingual education was used as intervention education that the Chicanitos needed in order to reach their level of capability. They were removed from their peers and were taught Spanish in an isolated situation which reinforced their negative feelings about themselves. Bilingual education has been a failure because it has been used as a tool for the disadvantaged to continue the perpetuation of the feeling that Chicanos have about themselves in the classroom. It becomes a matter of having Mexican-Americans doing it to Mexican-Americans.

Most of the professional bilingual teachers were taught by the University of Texas and UCLA. The history of bilingual education is interesting: it was a matter of the English teachers controlling the Chicanos, providing the leadership, and then training the Chicano teachers to use gringo models with their students.

•

RUBÉN ARMENDARIZ: I understand one of the difficulties that Chicanos face is a tremendous dropout rate. From 75 to 80 percent of Hispanics drop out of school. I'm a firm believer in education. I recall my father-in-law saying to me, "People can take away all the material things that you have, but the one thing they can't take away from you is your education. That is yours."

It's not that Chicanos or Hispanics do not believe in education; it's that education in this country is closely tied to economic means. You cannot divorce education from the economic condition of the country. All the school systems are built on a tax base. The system will only be as good as the tax base. So, a school system like Edgewood in San Antonio, which is a well-known situation, can have a tremendous number of taxable people. But the tax base is low because taxes are based on how much the property is worth. We measure the ability to educate a people on the economic basis and not necessarily on the ability. There is a definite correlation between economic means and education. Until we are able in this country to get over that, our people will always have difficulty. There is no equal opportunity for an education.

The whole thing is based on what you can afford. It is wrong, definitely wrong. You talk about a free educational system in the United States but there is nothing free about it. You talk about mass education but it isn't a mass educational system. It is some-get-less and some-get-better, depending on where your economic base is, or what the base can afford. But with that analysis you're going to be accused of being Marxist.

Violence and Nonviolence

Six of the Chicano leaders I interviewed opted for a nonviolent approach to our liberation. Three opted for any means necessary to protect ourselves against the Anglo-Saxons who continue to oppress us. From the nine responses, I chose three who opted for nonviolence and three for whatever means necessary to bring about our liberation.

The shared theme was stated as follows:

In our road to liberation we have two political and spiritual options. One option is nonviolence, the other is violence. Which option would you suggest for Chicanos in their struggle toward liberation and why?

JOSÉ ÁNGEL GUTIÉRREZ: I would opt for self-defense. I do not believe that nonviolence as a fixed policy is going to get us anywhere. If nothing else it will make us more subservient, more oppressed, and it will bring more brutalization to our community. I think we need to prepare to meet force with force. We need to defend our persons. We cannot speak of property rights because we have very little property. The only property we have is ourselves and that's the most valuable property that needs to be protected. I think that's the only position to take. Systematically, we have been the victims or targets of organized and directed violence. To take the position of nonviolence in face of that organized, directed conspiracy is to be totally irresponsible. I think we owe it to ourselves and to future generations to survive and to fight back. We need to set an example that we will continue to defend our positions.

•

DOLORES HUERTA: I think the only choice we have is nonviolence. If we resorted to violence we would be wiped out. Nonviolence is a spiritual strength. Going back to the Virgin of Guadalupe, to the whole of faith—in both, nonviolence has a strength and a power of its own. And you can measure that when you see the things you are able to accomplish with nonviolence. It is much stronger than violence. I call it a spiritual force. The people that are involved change. It even changes the enemy. It's a dynamic process.

•

RICARDO SÁNCHEZ: To be free means not to be a master or slave. If you want to take my freedom at one point, I must respond violently. I think that my responsibility to you is whatever degree of violence I need to defend myself. If they are oppressing me, then it is my responsibility to utilize any means whatsoever to bring about my liberation. I mean to utilize whatever force to whatever degree I need to. Need to! That's the key word to bring about my liberation. Therefore I cannot exclude violence.

Personally I would prefer a nonviolent, but expedient process. However, I will not fool myself into waiting around for a thousand years until the oppressor finally decides to give up oppressing me. So I'm saying whatever is needed to bring about liberation for our people is valid. Whatever is needed, no more than that and no less. Whatever course will succeed we must take.

The people who ask us to be gradualists, especially the oppressive types, don't want us to be complete because it would hurt them. They have vested interests. But the person who is hurting wants completion now, not a hundred years from now. I must do whatever I need to do to bring about some freedom. Realizing that, I think that freedom is a process. We will never ever be fully free, but we can at least be a little bit freer with each passing day.

•

TOMÁS ATENCIO: That's one of the simplest questions you have. It has to be nonviolence. But I am not so sure that it is nonviolence philosophically. It is nonviolence tactically. You can't win a violent struggle. It will destroy you. It's got to be done nonviolently, and it has got to be done symbolically.

Symbols, the phenomenological dimensions, are the ones that are going to help us out on this. This is why we can't let go of those aspects of our tradition that are related to our symbols. The reason I say this is because I see the gringo society has very few symbols that are rooted in the original myths, the primitive myths. They have a lot of symbols that are rooted in the kind of thing we call anachromyths. Myths that have developed around—say, Horatio Alger, or the flag. That is a symbol of a myth that is not a myth that goes that far back. It is a myth, but it's an anachromyth. It's a myth that has been put together around ideology mostly. It is not a myth that has been put together from a conscious human response to a national phenomenon, like fatalism, or love, or respect. This is where I come from. You have to go nonviolence.

•

REIES LÓPEZ TIJERINA: Well, I have no recommendation. It all depends upon the oppressor. It all depends on how badly you want to be liberated.

GUERRERO: But if you had a choice?

TIJERINA: I take it as it comes. I've had to make citizen's arrests in Tierra Amarilla where this is a legal constitutional right. But when we did it, the Anglos called it violence. Yet, they arrest millions of people and call it law and order. They don't like to be beaten at their own game. As soon as they lose, they change the rules and start all over again.

GUERRERO: So you're saying it's either/or?

TIJERINA: Yes, because there are two kinds of violence. Legal violence and unlawful violence. The Anglos used unlawful violence here to kill the Indians. In this case the Anglos were not on their land. They were on the land of the Indians.

Now if somebody comes here to abuse my family, I kill him. I kill him in my home because he is trying to rape, rob, or steal from my family. That is legal violence. The other kind of violence is if I go to someone else's home, enter, and kill somebody there. That's unlawful violence. We talk about the genocide of the Jews in Germany, who were not in their land. What about the genocide of Indians within their own land that continues up until today in America? Anglos committed unlawful violence in the land of the Indians.

GUERRERO: What about the conquistadores who came and killed the Indians?

TIJERINA: Okay, at least they had the sanction of the church, at least they had a document. They had international law protecting their coming, their crossing the Atlantic. That law was supported by England. All the rights of the nations derived from the triple crown of the pope. That triple crown was created by all the Catholic Christian nations.

•

RUBÉN ARMENDARIZ: Personally, I subscribe to a nonviolent position, that is to say, one can make confrontations and demands and attempt through a process to achieve a certain objective. Yet we need to define what violence is because violence is usually measured in terms of human harm or property harm. Violence is defined in terms of destroying property or injuring someone, physical harm. Yet, violence can take many shapes and forms which have nothing to do with harming someone physically. Violence can be a psychological thing.

If we talk in terms of violence, if I am for violence in the sense of pursuing justice, then I would opt for violence that is not harmful to the physical body or to property, but violence that shakes or confronts the status quo. One cannot rule out altogether physical violence.

People say that liberation theology sometimes advocates physical violence. They say that you're more for the leftists than you are for the rightists. If you are for the people, then you will support the leftists and that means providing arms, and that means killing people.

In our society here in the United States, as Chicanos, I think physical, harmful property violence is ridiculous. The reality that faces us is that we can be squashed in a minute. Let's say that two hundred brown berets decide that they are going to arm themselves and violently and physically react against the state capitol of Texas. What chance do you think they have? Immediately they will be squashed. A violent revolution in that sense would have no meaning. It's the same as saying "I'm going to go up against this institution (when it has a $20 million endowment and you have $10 in your pocket) and violently oppose it."

"Entre los individuos como entre las naciones,
el respeto al derecho ajeno es la paz"
("Between individuals as between nations,
respect for the rights of others is peace") [Benito Juárez]

Benito Juárez, statesman and president of Mexico, fought against the French occupation of Mexico in the 1860s. The above statement is one of his most famous. It is still quoted by many Chicanos in the barrios of the Southwest. I wanted to find out what our leaders thought about it. I stated the theme as follows:

> *Benito Juárez said:* "Entre los individuos come entre las naciones, el respecto al derecho ajeno es la paz." *Humanly speaking, what does this mean to Chicanos? Historically, have the United States government and the church abided by this norm? It would seem that the law of Christ is a law of respect, whether the respect is for the person or for the extension of the person in labor, art, culture, language, or religious beliefs. What are your reflections on Juárez's statement?*

RICARDO SÁNCHEZ: But I'm presupposing that respect is a mutual thing. If there is respect on both sides, there is peace. The problem with us is that neither the United States government, its institutions, nor the different churches and religious institutions that exist have respected the right of the Chicano to be Chicano.

•

TOMÁS ATENCIO: That's one of those feudal-era statements. But when you get out of that and into modern society, you need laws. I mean written laws that come out of common law and Roman law. "*El respeto al derecho ajeno es la paz*" is then plebeian law because there is no respect. That doesn't apply in Western industrial society because it is another kind of a system. I don't think that the United States or any other first world industrial country really goes by that. What they go by is constitutional government. That is what defines what *la paz* is. The peace is defined by constitutionality and within that are all kinds of values, all kinds of rhetoric. That statement of Juárez is very traditional. It comes out of traditional man and the *indiado* (Indianness). It comes out of a person who was a mixture of constitutionality and all kinds of other things.

I do believe in that statement, but it's just like the peasant statement in northern New Mexico, *mi casa es su casa*. That is another statement that is very feudal and very traditional. When those gringos from the East arrived here, they took it literally and they took the *casa*. When you look at what's happening today with that statement, most of your cities are being developed and your land is being developed around regional priorities that are not determined by the people who inhabit the land, but by the people that have the power.

GUERRERO: Economically?

ATENCIO: Yes, economically. That's why all of a sudden New Mexico becomes important. This is why the Sun Belt is so important. This is why New Mexico Chicanos stand to lose everything they have. But there's going to be a fight, though they stand to lose. Within this they are going to have some Chicanos jumping on the bandwagon saying, well, we're going to make a little bread out of it. If a guy wants to jump on that, he is still my friend. That doesn't make him bad or *vendido* [a sell-out] or anything. It's just that that's where he is at. So then, the next question: Is he a Chicano? Well, what is the definition of Chicano, or is it *raza*, which continually has to be redefined?

GUERRERO: I feel that if you sell out those traditions, values, and virtues that belong to a Chicano, you don't have a Chicano anymore.

ATENCIO: That is an interesting argument about what might be happening here.

We have to protect ourselves, that's the name of the game. But this idea of the peace, *el respeto a lo ajeno es la paz*, well, it is a very good concept, it's a very good statement, but it seems to be out of step with our time. It's out of step in the sense that the major powers have a different way of looking at things. To them respect is respect for the law, but then when you get back and understand who makes the laws, then you begin to see that this country is very close to being a corporative type of system. In other words, you have a small group of people who hold the power, and they are the ones who have the economic base and control the power. Then they say that public interest groups throughout the country are the ones that negotiate and are able to influence the Congress. Yes, they are, but even these little interest groups are still tied to the economic base. Even the Moral Majority, who represent a lot of midwesterners, a lot of southern farmers, a lot of people who are being displaced from their land, when you look at the last statement in their agenda, they support defense.

Then that raises the concern that they have no social program. That is bad. Yet they are using a symbol that is very important for all these people who have been dirt people.[7] This is where they are. But these dirt people fell into the clutches of those people who control the corporate structure. These people are patriotic; they have symbols such as, "Hey, one way to be patriotic is to support defense spending." When we look at that objectively, we are forced to ask what is going on with the Moral Majority supporting defense. Defense in this country really means a shift from welfare to warfare in terms of where the money goes. Those who benefit the most from a warfare state are the giant corporations like Lockheed, Dow Chemical, and other big electronic businesses.

•

REIES LÓPEZ TIJERINA: The father of that statement did not respect the rights of Indians. He took the land of the Indians. Let's stick to the reality of the fact. Property and the law we must respect. King Solomon said, "Respect the old boundary zone. Don't trespass it, never. Whether it's a widow, or an old man, or the poor, don't trespass it." I would rather listen to Solomon, one of our brothers, than to Benito Juárez, who was referring to Maximilian, who came here without respecting Mexico. Benito Juárez wanted political power; he wanted peace too, but he did not respect the rights of Indians. The father of that statement was a ruthless, gross transgressor against his own people. He was being used. I have no admiration for him.

The law and respect for private property I agree with because that's law. That's where we are strong and the Anglos are weak.

•

LUPE ANGUIANO: I believe that *"el respeto al derecho ajeno es la paz"* is a really profound Christian statement. The Catholic Church in dealing with us has never respected our language or our culture or our right to worship in our own historical experience.

I did a study of the Catholic Church in the Southwest. I went to New Mexico and spoke with a lot of parish priests about the right of people to worship within their language and their cultural experience. Among the things I found was that priests, if the parishioners wanted a Mass in Spanish, would relegate that Mass to either a Saturday night or Sunday at an hour that was so early in the morning that few would attend. The religious expression of Catholics has been very Irish, very Anglo. We had the Mass in the vernacular preference as expressed by Rome, but that was never really applied to our people. So many churches are a hundred percent Mexican-American or Spanish-speaking, particularly in the isolated places in New Mexico.

The interesting thing I found in New Mexico (perhaps that is the salvation of the faith) is that the priest can only go to a church once a month. On every other Sunday the people organize the liturgy. In the old days the people would elect a sacristan or a head person to get the people together. They would pray the rosary and conduct prayers in Spanish. Once a month the priest came and they had Mass. A lot of criticism is placed upon the *Penitentes* of New Mexico. But I believe that they are the salvation of our faith. The continuation of our faith in New Mexico does not have to do with the priests. It has to do with the faith of the people. A priest does his thing not realizing that for the people it's just motions that he is going through. The real faith is expressed in a totally different way.

In the study I made, one of the issues raised was the *altares* we have in the homes. We have altars because that is the only place where we can really express our faith, our belief, our liturgy. That is where we feel, on a real gut level, close to Christ. It isn't in the parish. It isn't in the church because a lot of that liturgy is so foreign. How can you feel? How can you really express faith, hope, and charity? Faith, hope, and charity are not only intellectual; they are also an emotional, social expression that involves the total being. I cannot express my faith with a liturgy at St. Mary's.

GUERRERO: I understand what you are saying. I always wondered: why all the *altares*?

ANGUIANO: That is why our faith is strong and alive in our community. It's because it's in the home.

GUERRERO: With the Black people it's in the spirituals, their songs, and the fact that, even though they were ousted, they still have a native clergy. For us the resistance has been the *altares*, the *Virgen de Guadalupe*, and the language. That has helped us survive.

ANGUIANO: Without that we probably would be either atheists or agnostics. If we really took seriously what the priest tells us in the church, we would have lost our faith.

The Land

Chicanos have a spiritual affinity with the land. Most of them have worked the land; many still work the land for a living. Nature, the woods, the forests, the streams, the lakes, *el campo* (the countryside), have always had a special place in the hearts of all Chicanos.

Traditionally on Easter the young, the old, everybody, *se van al campo* (go to the country). What better way to celebrate the day of the resurrection than through union with nature and *la tierra* (the land). So I believe that for us there is something sacred and spiritual about the land. Among other things the land is a strong symbol of the identity of a people.

The shared theme was stated as follows:

The question of the land is a very delicate one, because whoever controls the land controls the people living upon it. Nevertheless, the people have an affinity with the land that is almost sacred. New Mexicans have land grants which the U.S. government refuses to honor in spite of the Guadalupe-Hidalgo Treaty it made with Mexico in 1848. A large number of Chicanos are migrant workers who farm the land of agribusiness and multinationals. The growers get richer and the migrant workers get exploited and poorer. How does one reconcile the affinity of the land with the spirit of the people in the movement toward liberation? Is there a message here that we have not theologically or spiritually emphasized in order to break the chains of fatalism and inferiority, chains that hurt and destroy our people? How would you utilize this idea? Or is the idea good at all given the time in history and the Anglo-Saxon, who in reality occupies the land of our ancestors, both Indians and mestizos. Should this theme be

investigated for the purpose of liberating the spirit from its
oppressive counterparts? Emiliano Zapata's revolutionary
motto was Tierra y Libertad. *What does this mean for Chica-*
nos sixty years later?

JOSÉ ÁNGEL GUTIÉRREZ: Regrettably, it doesn't mean a
thing because of the history books that completely rewrote history
and erased that portion of the question addressing the rightful heirs
and owners of these lands. The federal occupation of lands in New
Mexico and other places of occupied Mexico is not taught in the
American schools. Our kids, all kids, grow up believing this is the
American country, always has been, always will be. They believe
that the founding of this country took place at Plymouth Rock by
white Pilgrims and thirteen colonies, that everything that is American is white and is attributed to white persons of a certain Nordic
stock and that *stands*. We have lost touch with our historical roots,
our land roots. Emiliano Zapata's motto was applicable to the state
of Morelos for a definite reason. We will need a different motto.

The conditions are the same, though. As county judge, I can tell
you that when we go through the tax rolls and we look at ownership
patterns, we find that twenty-six persons or corporations own 87
percent of the land here in Zavala County. In Maverick, which is a
border county in Eagle Pass, ten people own 91 percent of the land.
If you compare that kind of disproportion to the state dictatorships
of El Salvador, Somoza's Nicaragua, Ecuador, Bolivia, or Batista's
Cuba, then what we have is colonization. If you fly over communities like Pharr you'll see that they're big plantations. What we have
is just a little village where people live in huts. But the property
itself is just an outline. Everything else is farmland for maybe
twenty to thirty miles and then the woods take over again.

But things can't change because we don't have the means to buy
that land. We cannot push a *tierra y libertad* movement here. We
would be killed instantly. There's not going to be any land reform
just like there hasn't been any land reform in many of the revolutionary countries. In fact, the Mexican Revolution was betrayed
for lack of following through on agrarian reform.

The redistribution of wealth is a fundamental question. In this
country even the liberals believe in equal opportunity but that in
itself is an unfair position to take because we are not on equal

grounds to begin with. What we need is equality in the distribution of wealth, and that will never happen. There even our liberal friends would desert us because what you need here is a full-scale revolution. I don't see that occurring any time soon.

During urban renewal, Chicanos fought fiercely because of their identity with certain parts of land such as the cemetery and the place of birth. In northern New Mexico you find that same affinity, but that attachment goes beyond the cemetery and the birthplace to inheritance, to land grants, and to knowing that our land has been taken from us. New Mexicans have continued to farm. We haven't done that. We just work on the farms that belong to the masters. We have had such horrible experiences.

We have also been unsuccessful with federal programs and with banks. Everything is made available to us except the opportunity to purchase land. We have tried to buy a thousand acres to set up a Chicano cooperative. The governor fought us; the local politicians fought us; everybody fought us. We couldn't do it. We tried organizing a few people to get something together but it couldn't be done. We couldn't get the holdings in large enough numbers.

•

MSGR. LONGINUS REYES: I think that the ownership of land in relation to people is an enormous topic. It's essential for a person to own land. Land gives identity, a meaning to life. It is the mother of existence and to me that's what it's all about. You fight for your land; you do everything for your land. This concept has been used in the past wars of this country and of other nations to alarm its populace to defend its land.

I think the concept of identity of the people with the land is a reality. We don't really need to discuss the significance of the land to the people. Certainly I think in our Mexicano experience the struggles—the fight for liberation, the Wars for Independence in Mexico—indicate a strong tie to the land. When you control the land, you control the destiny of the people.

By the acquisition or owning of the land the person or a nation of people have something with which to identify. Their whole existence—ceremonies, religion, everything—is based on *su Dios*, *su vida* (their God, their life). It's interesting that in this country we always say there is a separation of church and state. But religion influences, it permeates, the sphere of politics. Why does the whole morality issue come into politics at this time? It is because the people of the United States are afraid of the disintegration of values and of the "American way of life." But what they're really afraid of is the Soviet Union's potential as a superpower to take away *nuestra tierra*.

The whole political presidential campaign was very interesting because there was no difference between the candidates' platforms. If there was a difference, it was one made by religion around the threat of losing the land. What was coming through was that we're getting to be less and less powerful in the world, which means we're going to lose influence and eventually going to lose our land. The other superpowers can take it away from us. That's what it's all about. So we're really not that concerned about the disintegration of values and morality. What we're really concerned with is how these values and morality affect the defense of this land, which others can take away from us. At least that's what I see.

GUERRERO: By land do you mean property and material interest?

REYES: It is more than property and material interest. When you have a piece of land you build something upon it. Whatever it is you build materially there symbolically brings out your spiritual values. Even the shape or the architecture of your home or your business reflects your values. It's kind of an intriguing concept that within that land is who you are. When you lose that land you lose everything. Displaced people are dispossessed of their values, of their heritage, of their religion, and of their life.

That is why in the Exodus event what really upset the Israelites was their wandering in the desert. As they searched for the promised land they also were seeking for an identity as a people. Their values, their religion, their heritage, their history, their God, their everything was based on the promised land. As long as they were wandering in the desert, they were nomads; they were nobodies. That's why I think that when you take the land away from people, they will either give their lives for it or else they will just be nobodies. You destroy them. They become passive. They cease to exist.

Fatalistic and Anarchistic Tendencies

Because of our oppression and because of our traditions we Chicanos have *dichos* (sayings) that are fatalistic in meaning. *Así lo manda Dios*; *si Dios quiere*; *ya le tocaba*[8]—these are a few of them. We have been accused by the dominant gringo society of being anarchistic. But the gringo society has failed to listen to us and to understand our Chicano worldview. It has been their worldview we have had to assimilate because they felt conquest justified it.

The shared theme was stated as follows:

Virgilio Elizondo has said that Chicanos, like other oppressed groups, have fatalistic traits. Leo D. Nieto says that we have been accused of having anarchistic tendencies. Are these valid criticisms? What about our hopes and cosmovisions of mutuality and equality for all human beings? The rich, it seems, strive for individuality; the poor strive for mutuality. Is individuality a luxury the poor cannot afford or will the poor really inherit the earth as the cosmic Christ predicted they would?

JOSÉ ÁNGEL GUTIÉRREZ: I have respect for Mr. Elizondo and Mr. Nieto, both of whom I know. But I differ with them. It is not anarchy to fight and rebel against what you perceive to be negative things. For example, our community is called apathetic when it comes to voting. Apathy, if you think about it, implies a choice not to do something. I don't know if we have a choice about anything. I think the most appropriate word for us is cynical because the system is built for someone else, not us. You sometimes hear people say the system doesn't work. People couldn't be more wrong. The system works very well for what it's intended to do. It is not intended to work for us. So this is the beginning point of my answer.

What we see out here is the frustration, the bitterness, the high incidence of alcoholism, and the vicious cannibalism among ourselves. On the surface it may appear that we're in total anarchy, total chaos. These are just the manifestations of underlying problems, of being landless, voteless, powerless, and impotent. My God, that's humiliating.

That's as bad as not having a job. In not having a job you can't prove yourself; you can't have dignity when you're unemployed, when you're on food stamps, when you can't feed your kids, when you can't look them in the eye and say, "I'm going to take you for a soda pop, or I'm going to buy you a little race car." God, that just robs you of everything. Poverty is the most depressing situation to be in. And it is not authorized by ourselves. We are mandated to be locked into that situation by a host of problems—an insensitive and inequitable educational system that keeps us potential pushouts, an economic system that only wants us as laborers. Now they have invented programs to train us to accept low wages and unemployment as a state of life. That's the CETA program. We have subsidized unemployment now. And that's what we've done for the last six, seven years.

I could go on and on. The gerrymandering is an example of all that. I don't think that we're anarchic. I think that what we're seeing is the beginnings of a people becoming aware of what is happening. They are organizing themselves as best they can, are beginning to deal with each other and to mobilize around certain things that are important to them.

•

TOMÁS ATENCIO: I have to talk about northern New Mexico. It is important because it was one of the areas that survived the onslaught of gringos and Mexicans. The uniqueness of New Mexico is that the Spanish influence still survives there. It is also important because of the land base. The people there have always been anarchistic.[9] I don't think it is an accusation. I think it is a compliment. The kind of anarchism that prevails in northern New Mexico is not the kind of political anarchism that came out of the twenties. The northern New Mexicans were peasant anarchists. They were people who had a direct relationship to the land. They had no *patrón* (boss). They worked for themselves. There were some that had more than others, but basically, they subsisted off the land.

Okay, this kind of peasant anarchy was not an ideological anarchy. It was an anarchy that gave you the freedom to be a people of the land, a people of nature. This is a heritage that was handed down to us. The *indios* also were anarchists and at the same time they had a sense of communality. Look at the mutual aid societies that came into this country from Mexico. They were getting together because of economic necessity. But there was also another thing there. That is that they are not contradictory. They appear contradictory. You can be an anarchist and at the same time be together because of the kind of anarchism that you have.

GUERRERO: Why do you think the gringos accuse Chicanos of anarchism? Why do they criticize so vehemently an anarchism they don't understand?

ATENCIO: Well, I think that, really, coming from a non-Chicano that would be racist. To say that you are anarchistic, I would consider that a compliment. To them it is surely not a compliment. To them they are saying: you're not with us. Because if we were with them, we would be with them on their own terms. Anarchism, from the point of view that I am speaking, means that we will be with you, but on *our* terms. Once you say that, you're an anarchist.

But to say that we will be with you, but we want to be on our terms whatever we are, that is the kind of anarchism that has prevailed among Chicanos. Chicanos were able to find some communality, when they had to, around the most important things like death and birth. This is where folklore and myth connect to become one.

For example, what does the *compadrazgo* system mean? Well, it has a well-defined social function. If your father dies, your godfather takes care of you. And your *compadre* is going to help you in everything that is economic. But also who is the one who witnesses baptism? Who is the one who witnesses marriage? Who is the one who witnesses death if he is still alive? Your godfather. So there you have the *compadrazgo* of folklore tied to the myth in religion, tied to the socioeconomic structure. If you look at it that way, then how can you accuse us. I mean you can be anarchist within that because you're still going to be a people of the land, independent, but at the same time you're going to be communal. Now whenever Chicanos were anarchistic, like the *Penitentes* of New Mexico,[10] they were persecuted. The *Penitentes* had a social control that was very effective.

GUERRERO: Yes, but it was a threat to the structure outside that was trying to break it up.

ATENCIO: Of course, because if you control your own brotherhood through the kind of punishment the *Penitentes* used to inflict, that builds your brotherhood even stronger. If you were really bad during Holy Week they would kill you.

Those are very viable things; that's a phenomenon that has been around. The industrial revolution has been around for many years. The coming-out of the feudal society into modernized society has been around since the twelfth or thirteenth century so what happens is that there seems to be a phenomenon that certain groups that don't give in develop into anarchistic groups, into social banditry, into those kinds of things that become deviant as viewed by the dominant but are not deviant at all if viewed by the society within. I think you have those kinds of things, so that's why they would say, he is an anarchist. That means he is a deviant. Well, to us it is a compliment.

GUERRERO: What about the fatalism?

ATENCIO: Well, I don't consider fatalism that derogatory in the face of an aggressive system that says that you manipulate your own environment and your own destiny and produce the present. This is similar to what we find in the Scriptures: God created human beings and then they have control of all nature. I think that's the thing that is going to kill this earth. So whenever they say you are fatalistic, you can come back and say yes, but you are murderers. Why? Because you believe in control over nature, where we believe in harmony with nature.

Fatalism is a kind of value. Myth comes out of energy like matter comes out of energy. The variable that creates myth is consciousness. So when early humans heard thunder, lightning struck and started a fire. They looked at it, consciously. Their first reaction was: there is something I don't understand. Around that some things begin to fall together, some little molecules that we call values.

So fatalism would be an acceptance of that which happens. It's a primitive belief system because you have no control over it. Many would say as you learn more about society you become more conscious of it. Fatalism is an acceptance of your destiny. I think that is positive. It also means a worldview in which you are in harmony with nature. Now let's ask: Could you have developed an industrial society with that type of value system? You could, but I think you would have respect for certain things. Of course to us we didn't see our land raped that much by mining here in New Mexico. When you look at that, you say: Is that what they did over there, is that what they are going to do over here until it is all over? What is it that they are doing? Well, certainly that is the example of the opposite of fatalism because fatalism is something that flows out of our harmony with nature.

GUERRERO: So it's not so much the detachment from reality but accepting reality as it really is.

ATENCIO: Yes, as it is.

GUERRERO: So it depends on how one sees this concept, *"así lo manda Dios."* We can use that as positive energy or negative energy force.

ATENCIO: Many people have used *"así lo manda Dios"* because they have no alternative. They accept their reality as it is. They accept their destiny. Why? Because it's historic. It's within a big picture.

The Catholic Church: Sacrament of Liberation or Opium of the People?

My purpose in sharing this theme was to discover how our Chicano leaders felt about the Catholic Church. For some time now, many Chicano Catholics have been leaving the Catholic Church. Many are becoming Pentecostals, Baptists, and Mormons. I feel that the major reasons why Chicanos are leaving relate to our oppressed situation, to the lack of sensitivity (*corazón*) on the part of the institutional church, and to the lack of a native Chicano clergy.

The shared theme was stated as follows:

Many Chicanos have left the church or have joined Protestant churches because the Catholic Church has refused to face the real issues that affect the needs of the Chicano community; others have remained to work for changes in the life and destiny of the Chicanos. What are your thoughts concerning the Catholic Church in the lives of Chicanos?

JOSÉ ÁNGEL GUTIÉRREZ: I divide the church into two groups. I'm one of the disaffected Catholics. By disaffected I mean that I was in the church for a long time. I received the sacraments in the church. And then I got thoroughly disgusted with the things I'm going to talk about. In every one of these little communities where we're so wretched, the church comes and oppresses us more, with the collections, with the poor missionary work in Africa or in South America. The missionary work needs to be done right here. The social needs and ills that are here are the ones that need to be addressed. The church needs to get off our backs. I find the business of the church totally repulsive. The politics of the church, the personnel of the church, is totally alien to my being. We have more colonizers—Irish, Germans, Spaniards, and Italians— ministering to our spiritual needs in their own way.

Spelling out the dogma to reinforce the status quo is just no different from what the local newspaper does and what the local television does and what the local grower does. Everybody takes a little piece of the action to keep us in our place. During Lent is the only time a missionary Mexicano comes to speak to the Chicanos so as to give us a spiritual uplift, to rejuvenate us, and to get us back in line. That's when you get all fired up and you're ready to go because you have become a militant for Jesus. After Lent has passed, you're right back to the rough times. You're told it's good to be in misery, to offer it up, to say ten Hail Marys, to make the first nine Saturdays, and so forth.

Well, every decade or so the propaganda changes. Before we could buy indulgences, then we could do nine Saturdays and nine Fridays. Now I don't know what the latest gimmick is. But the point is that the gringo priest ought not to tell us to be content with our misery. There is no admonition for the rich other than the parable of the camel going through the eye of the needle before the rich get to the gates of heaven. Raising the awareness of the rich who are responsible for the misery through the unjust wages and horrible conditions is not mentioned at all.

I can dream of the church as an activist Christian movement— that could be the most beautiful thing possible. To have the person- nel, to have the power, to have the business, to have the politics of the church on the side of the poor, the downtrodden, God almighty, nobody could stop us. But to have this crusade, this born-again Christian movement, the new morality, all being attributed to Christianity, I find that hypocritical. I am just overwhelmed. I can't deal with that.

The messages, the ten commandments, the sound advice, the common sense, the good direction—all that to me is beautiful. I have tried to apply those principles to myself in my own private being and with my family. I find great satisfaction when I do that. I find myself a lesser man when I violate those principles because they're a good rule of conduct to follow. But I don't think we need to go to buildings to listen to the personnel who have other interests in mind, or to hear about the needs of the church in Latin America, in Asia, in Africa, throughout the world, and neglect the needs here in the Chicano barrios. We don't need to hear a review of the organized church, or the business of the church, or the politics of the church, which has always aligned itself with the governing class and never with the governed.

I don't think the dogma is an opium if it is lived as it is preached. Christianity could be the most powerful movement, as it has proved itself to be in the last several centuries. For Chicanos, it may be the only movement left for us.

•

MSGR. LONGINUS REYES: I think that to effect any kind of change in society or in the lives of people, an individual or a group of persons has to do it through systems or institutions. All kinds of changes that have come about came because of the impact on institutions that are affecting the lives of others. I was discussing with a friend how the ERA (Equal Rights Amendment) program was trying to effect changes in attitudes by working within an institution. It doesn't matter whether the institution is formal or informal. There is something positive about working within an institution that is instrumental in bringing about changes. I think you have to have an impact on the institution.

I think the Catholic Church as an institution within society can have a tremendous impact on the lives of peoples, especially on the lives of Chicanos. The other day I was discussing with a friend the ordination of women in the Episcopal Church. She said, "You see how the Episcopal Church did it. When is the Catholic Church going to ordain women?" The Episcopal Church is a very select group of people. That is why it doesn't take much to change that institution. Now, if the Catholic Church ordains women, it is going to have an impact. The Catholic Church takes in everybody. The Episcopal Church is economically and educationally one group. But the Catholic Church takes people from all the strata from the very poor to the very rich, from the educated to the uneducated; then it's going to have an impact on many people. However, the problem with that is that the broader the impact, the harder it is to change. That kind of change takes a longer time. Once it happens, though, that type of impact creates change.

I personally believe that both Protestant churches and the Catholic Church use the Chicanos. The Chicanos are being victimized by the Protestant churches in their whole evangelization process. What are Baptists or Mormons or Pentecostals going to do when they have all the Chicanos? Then they are going to have to respond to the Chicanos. Right now they don't have to respond as the Catholic Church is beginning to respond to the Chicano. The Chicanos haven't really said to the Roman Church, to the Baptist Church, or to the Episcopal Church, "Here we are, now you deal with us because this is what we need and this is what we want." We just haven't done that. I don't expect the institution itself to respond. Institutions never do that. They don't identify needs and respond to them. That just never happens. The only thing we can hope to do is just keep banging away at it, keep chipping away at it until it responds to our needs. When you begin to define those needs in terms of more Chicano personnel, more clergy, more resources, more money, more education, more attention to our problems, then I think the Roman church has no other avenue but to respond either positively or negatively, but it can't remain luke-warm to Chicanos.

Theologically, I think the church is a sacrament of liberation. Practically, it is a different question altogether. I think within the Catholic Church there is a need for structural change. I don't want to get into statistics because we all know there's no Chicano representation within the Catholic Church. By that I mean real representation. I'm not talking about x number of Chicano bishops or x number of Chicano priests.

We used to fight with the Austin Police Department about recruiting Chicano police officers; we stopped very quickly with that game because if these Chicano police officers didn't have their heads screwed on right, then it was worse than not having any

Chicano police officers. You have got to have the right people, and you have got to have them in the right positions. If you're going to have the responsibility, you have got to have the authority. That is what we need. We need people who have a sense of who they are as a Chicano people and who have the authority. We went through the token routine in the sixties. That is all over. I think that if the church wants to be authentic and genuine to the Chicano people, it has to do away with tokens, symbolic representation, and window dressing. I think the church is the one institution whose responsibility is to be genuine. It has got to be genuinely concerned for the Chicano people.

But I'm more concerned with what's happening to the Chicano people as they're being used by the churches. At one extreme of the spectrum is the Jehovah's Witnesses, who are splitting up our families and creating all kinds of problems. At the other extreme is the Catholic Church, not genuinely enough concerned about our needs as a Chicano people. In between these two extremes are all the other churches, condoning and legitimizing in their own particular way the situation of Chicano oppression.

•

TOMÁS ATENCIO: Well, I think that the Catholic Church in years back was responsible for the Chicanos' oppression. When Bishop Lamy first came here, he was responsible for destroying the native priesthood. Then there was a gap of some eighty years before a native priest was ordained. I think his name was Meléndez. So you can see that since 1850 there has been a black-out. That means that the Catholic Church, by not developing the native priesthood, was really imposing something from the outside. At the same time the Chicano people were able to keep their faith. They kept their faith because they had the *Penitentes* and other kinds of secular orders. They kept it together by a deep faith, tied to such things as agriculture, folklore, and fatalism.

The Catholic Church was responsible for their oppression, but on the other hand, it was also the institution the people looked to as their spokesperson. Right here, the Jesuits managed this church up until 1967. In 1880 when New Town was developed, this town became a rural village. It was very poor from 1880 to 1945. The

only thing that kept the people alive was their folklore, their
subsistence lore, and traditional beliefs. The New Town people
laughed at the Chicanos as *supersticiosos*. But that was what kept
them alive; plus *Jesucristo* was here, and economically they were
able to keep the church alive.

At the same time the Jesuits were the ones who brought the
Sisters of Charity, who created the San Felipe School. The first
school in Albuquerque was in the Chicano town. Who went to
school there? Chicanos. Who supported this church in spite of their
poverty? Chicanos. The church supplied. You know we have to
look at those things too.

So even though they were religious priests and not diocesan, they
made a lot of changes. Then the time came in the mid-sixties when
they were going to tear down the church and build it like in 1706.
Luis Jaramillo, who was vice-chancellor, became pastor and
stopped that. He also warned about what commercialization was
doing to this town. Here before you there were all residences. Not
too long ago, my wife remembers going into all these houses to see
people.

So you see the church does have a history of oppression, but it
also has a history of liberation. I see that you have enlightened men
and women within the traditional Catholic Church. The folk Catholic Church ties in to mystery, to myth, and to symbols. In getting
enlightened men and women in touch with those traditional things
the church has managed to survive.

So when you come up with folk Catholicism, when you come up
with things that are not quite modernized, like tradition, myths,
and symbols, you contribute to the church that is together with the
thinkers, with the people who are enlightened, reflecting, and
thinking. The Catholic Church is probably the only hope for
Chicanos, if we can get together that folk Catholicism with the
church that is enlightened, reflecting, and thinking.

If we can tie in those traditional roots of folk Catholicism to a
theology of liberation and to the social sciences, we are going to be
in a better position to understand the world.

Theology

Theology was the last theme that I shared with the Chicano
leaders. I asked about it because we Chicanos do not have a

theology that addresses our needs from the perspective of our own experience. The liberation theologies of Africa, Black America, Latin America, and Asia have been closely scrutinized and insensitively attacked by the dominant European white Christian theology that ecclesiastically aided in the conquest, colonization, and occupation of these oppressed peoples. Because this theme is so important, I include here all nine responses.

The shared theme was stated as follows:

> *Theology in Latin America, Black America, Asia, and Africa has until recently been written from the perspective of the conqueror-colonizer. In theory this perspective always expounded universal truths and categories. In practice, however, it always left out the voices of the people of different colors. This theology always addressed and sought to meet the needs of those colonizing instead of those being colonized. Hence, its cosmic vision was lacking; its universal categories were never developed enough to include the voice of those being oppressed. Instead of an inclusive cosmic totality, there existed only a partial totality.[11] Hence, the complete problem and need were not entertained in the discussion and research. In other words, the dominant theology left out those who were oppressed. Instead, it addressed the needs of the oppressor and colonizer. From our own experience, what would such a theology teach us?*

JOSÉ ÁNGEL GUTÍERREZ: I disagree with the statement the way it's worded because I think there are two churches; there are two theologies. The dominant theology is on the side of the governing class, of the social economic elites. That tendency developed a long time ago when the popes were part of the political powers of the world. The pope divided the world into a domain for Spain, a domain for Portugal, and for other Catholic countries. Aside from the theological questions and points to redefine, Protestantism developed as a protest against Catholic dominance and overbearance.

The political questions are obvious. Catholics, through the pope, determined what was happening in the world in order to get a piece of the action. Protestants began their empire building starting with

Luther and followed by different sects and other denominations. I don't think that is undermining the basis, the essence of the political question. The politics of the church, the business of the church has aligned itself with those social, economic elites. I don't think that has changed.

I'm not questioning the fundamental work of the priest or nun working in the slums of Latin America, or in the African villages, or in a barrio in the Southwest, who has opted to defend the poor like Camilo Torres in Colombia, Ernesto Cardenal in Nicaragua, Archbishop Oscar Romero in San Salvador, and Bishop Mendez Arceo in Cuernavaca, Mexico. These representatives are with the poor church. Now it depends on what church you are talking about; that is why the question to me is worded in such a way that I would disagree.

GUERRERO: What I'm referring to here is the theology that we're taught in schools, in seminaries, and in universities.

GUTIÉRREZ: That's why I say it is a white theology.

GUERRERO: What can that theology teach us?

GUTIÉRREZ: It can teach us who the enemy is and who the messengers and businessmen are.

•

MSGR. LONGINUS REYES: Very simply, it has taught us how to pray, in the sense of not doing anything about our situation. I mean it hasn't taught us about our condition as oppressed and what to do about that oppression. It's the whole process of coming to a liberation from this oppression. But in a way I would say it has taught us to pray.

GUERRERO: What do you mean, it has taught us to pray?

REYES: If you have a problem you go pray, but you never really become conscious of the problem or what's causing that problem or how to work at resolving that problem. Hell, that's all we've done is pray. All the way through we've prayed and prayed. People come to us with problems and we say, "Well, pray to God; God's going to take care of it." But it never brings a consciousness to people of their oppression, of what the elements are, of the institution, of the factors, and of the complexity of what's oppressing them. It doesn't even make them aware that they're oppressed.

GUERRERO: So it's really not an authentic prayer, is it?

REYES: No, not by any means. An authentic prayer would be a recognition of the situation. Like the prayer of Moses, who was angry about the situation and did something about it. Bad prayer is an opium. It is a negative thing because it doesn't help one to work out of the situation; it doesn't teach one to fight; it has no vision, no hope. It's a dead situation. Like a prophet, prayer should do two things. It should destroy, but it should also resurrect. There ought to be an awareness of what needs to be changed and a hope and a vision of something new coming into being.

GUERRERO: So you would say that we need a theology that relates to the situation and not one that alienates us from the situation?

REYES: Yes. Theology has definitely given us a lot of data. What Thomas Aquinas systematized has been taught to us, but what has not been taught to us is that we are God's people; we are persons who share in the creative power of God and the redemptive power of God. We're redeemers, co-creators together with Christ, who unites our suffering, our passion, our death to make together with him a creature and a redemptive situation. Theology has not been redemptive because it hasn't brought and redeemed the people from their condition of sin, which is that oppressive situation they live in. Rather it has alienated people from themselves and from their God.

•

BISHOP CHÁVEZ: They say that European theology has been brought into all other areas of the world. The European theology reflects the intellectuals and the history of Europe more than other nations. It doesn't reflect the needs of the non-European nations and how they relate to God and to society in all the aspects of life. That's very true. That doesn't mean it is completely wrong. It served its purpose because it preserved faith and it preserved the Bible and other traditions. But it doesn't mean in any way that it is perfect.

Truth must be sought. It is an ongoing process. I guess that theology is not totally irrelevant because liberation in its emphasis is a new concept. They thought they possessed the truth and other people didn't. But now we know that all cultures and all societies have many truths in their own way of looking at life and that no culture is superior to another. Culture becomes part of religion. What they were saying was that European culture was superior to other cultures.

The concept of liberation had been lost for centuries—even though it is contained in the Bible. The concept of liberation had not been applied to many areas of life. In the Bible it is just connected to slavery, physical slavery. But now liberation can be applied to many other kinds of enslavement. Now liberation has come to mean an awareness. I think liberation is an advancement of civilization. Lots of people have become aware. Not that everyone is aware; lots of people don't even know the concept. The ordinary working person, the ordinary working American, doesn't even know what it means. A lot of people don't understand liberation, and therefore it cannot be applied to them. Even our Chicano people, not all of them know. All some know is advancement and success. But they're not aware of liberation.

GUERRERO: They are aware of what the colonizer wants them to be aware of.

BISHOP CHÁVEZ: Yes, that's true.

GUERRERO: What do you think the job of the intellectual is then: Is it to get the message to the people?

BISHOP CHÁVEZ: Well, to those who want to hear. The prophetic role is to influence the people in authority and power. In other circumstances, the consciousness of the people in general is influenced, as it is being done in Latin America. There they are not going to the power but are going to the people. But here in the United States the task is so big, the only ones who could do something are the people in power. And gradually also the people at the grassroots, but that takes suffering people. They have to be aware of the suffering. The big problem here in the United States is that people are not politically aware of their suffering; therefore as long as they are not, they are not concerned about liberation.

GUERRERO: Do you think the people are happy and that's why they won't move?

BISHOP CHÁVEZ: Yes, that's the whole problem. As long as people have the materialistic things they want, their furthest interest is liberation for all.

•

DOLORES HUERTA: When you talk about religion, it is still a political issue, especially when you talk about the history of *La Raza Cósmica* or the history of the Chicano. Religion has been a very political thing for the Mexican. Look at the ancient Aztec religions: the reason the Indians helped the Spaniards overthrow the Aztecs was because the Aztecs were oppressing them. For them it was a liberation because they wanted to get back at the Aztecs. So you could say that the Catholic religion unified and organized the Indians.

Another interesting thing that you mention is the theology of the conqueror. The Protestant religion is worse than the Catholic religion in terms of the native Americans. The Catholic religion believes in baptism, so if you baptized people then you gained their souls. The Protestant religion was very color-oriented so it just wiped the native Americans out.

You see the differences between the United States and Mexico. In Mexico the *indios* still exist. In the United States they were wiped out. So in a way we were lucky that we were conquered by the Catholics instead of by the Protestants. Protestant politics were genocidal, whereas Catholics converted the heathen by baptism. I'm not saying that the Catholics did not kill a lot of Indians; they did. But they didn't wipe out the tribes the way they did in North America.

When I was in New York City, during the boycott, I'd see people go down to the Lower East Side and the Lower West Side to hear Mass. The churches were filled with people from Mexico and South America. The Puerto Rican churches were also full. The priests would get up there and talk about how many angels you could put on the head of a pin. I mean they wouldn't talk about anything political. The sermons were not relevant to the politics affecting the people's lives.

The priests, nuns, and seminarians should be with the poor people because you can't understand or even respect the poor unless you live their lives. You can't talk about a theology of liberation without political activism; you've got to be politically involved at every level. Otherwise, you lose the poor.

•

RICARDO SÁNCHEZ: Theology teaches us to feel diminished. A new theology of liberation, true liberation, would be all-inclusive, would perhaps give people the sense of destiny and dignity that they need, the psychological and spiritual reinforcements that they are lacking, the reflection that human beings are human and that they all have the right to thrive, to enjoy, to love, and that they are all not only capable of loving but worthy of being loved.

If it were to be manifested at first philosophically and theoretically in a real way, in a positive sense, then it would later become manifested via actions. And of course it would be transformative. It would be a transformative visualization; it would be a vision that would really be transformative because people would be able to act upon it in a spiral way. It would lead people to *concientización*, wherein people would be able to define their reality, to analyze and to reflect upon the analysis, and to act; people would be able to go back to definitions or redefinitions or superdefinitions. It would be part of becoming a more complete human being.

Also if we were to go away from the Western concepts of the demarcated human—you know, the mind is here, the soul is here, the body is there, which is the way the West approaches religion—its implications would be tranquilistic in all spheres of human activity. It would be rebelistic; the person would be dealt with in a total sense. All the different needs in a person could come to light and all the different resources in a person could come to create an illumination that would be really transformative. I believe that if people actually were to take this type of pain into their hands, they would learn to have a good sense of themselves. I think that the greatest fault in modern society is that we permit our institutions to get away from us. But let's be truthful, the church was never an institution in the hands of the people. Historically it never has been that.

Of course many theological people would condemn me for saying that, but I have never seen any of them walk the streets. There is a Latin American protest song that says: "There is something much more important on earth than God and that is that no one should spit blood so that another can thrive and live well." In another song, a young boy asks his grandfather: "Grandfather, what do you know of God?" His grandfather said, "He is having breakfast with the boss."

That's beautiful music out of Latin America that speaks about a reality that we don't know yet. That reality is anger, strength, beauty, indomitability, and power. I must say, also, that some of that music was created by priests who had courage, who were human, who were real, and who were friends of humanity with resistance, with the *pueblo*. So I cannot negate the value of those people, but those are a few people; the institution is vast and outnumbers them by millions.

•

TOMÁS ATENCIO: The best way to look at it is from a Marxist perspective. Marx said that Protestantism is the religion of the emergent bourgeoisie. Weber comes around and authenticates that. Marx would say that the economic base is what influences your ideology. The bourgeoisie, the merchants were developing. Who controlled the Catholic Church? The feudal system controlled the Catholic Church; the lords and the peasants were right in it. Then when the merchants began to develop, they needed a theology that would support individualism, one to one, justification by faith, you to God. Out of that you see Protestantism emerge. Protestantism was a good religion for the bourgeoisie.

GUERRERO: But isn't it strange that in most Catholic countries, for instance, Italy, where the Vatican is, there exists the lowest per capita income in the whole of Europe. In Latin America, where the majority are Catholics, you see a lot of poverty. I'm not trying to knock down the Catholics, but I'm trying to show something about Catholicism that ties in to a subservient poverty.

ATENCIO: You still have the thing coming out of the feudal system.

GUERRERO: You wait for the decision to come from the *patrón*, the bishop, in order to move.

ATENCIO: It's isomorphic. You find it in life; you find it in religion; and you find it in your concept of God. So you have it in the Catholic Church, whereas in the Protestant Church you have a bourgeoisie out of those that developed the world. Today the theology that has come to be the real influence in this world has been the one from the industrialized nations.

What was their theology to begin with? It was really the Protestant perspective. It even infiltrated the Catholic Church in some areas in this country. So that's why the theology that comes down from Germany or the continent or the theology that is developed here is a theology that reflects the conditions of the majority and is used as the justification for those who are in control. That is what it tells us: that theology is the ideology of the people who are in control. It's the religious ideology of the people who control, and we don't have an ideology. The people who are oppressed have no ideology. Why? Because of all the things you asked me before. Education has not allowed us to put it together. We have not had the printing press. We haven't had the resources to put it together—the intellectual resources, as well as the physical resources to put together a theology of the oppressed. So a theology of the oppressed has to be developed that speaks from the side of the poor.

•

REIES LÓPEZ TIJERINA:

GUERRERO: What will that theology teach us? The theology that . . .

TIJERINA: Oppresses the poor and helps the few?

GUERRERO: Well, they don't say "Don't help the poor." They say "Help everybody."

TIJERINA: Well, corruption in the church and discrimination exists like it exists in politics because the church government is almost identical to the political governments. Just as the government gets corrupted, so the church gets corrupted. Once it is corrupted, then the leaders discriminate. Those are the human, earthly weaknesses, for which we cannot condemn the authority established by Christ. The church, the covenant, that is clean. There is corruption, there is evil, but it is human.

Because of corruption, the church has failed on many occasions. The church in the Old Testament murdered and killed the prophets. But you don't find a prophet, Amos, Isaiah, or Ezekiel, coming to a covenant church and priesthood saying I'm going to tear down this organization, this church institution, and build a new one. No, all they did was rebuke, criticize, and tell the priests to regenerate, to reform, to do better, but they would never challenge the authority vested in the priesthood.

The same thing in the New Covenant. We can rebuke; we can criticize the church, but we cannot challenge the authority vested in the priesthood by Christ. Therefore when the church created the title it was performing a duty. Christ told Peter whatever you bind on earth shall be bound in heaven. Pope Alexander VI, by his authority, made the title of America for Spain. That is holding; that is binding. It was the pope's authority. Nobody had given the Anglos any right in America. None whatsoever. They built it themselves. They build their rights by dropping out of the church and creating a new religious authority.

•

LUPE ANGUIANO: Your reward is going to be great in heaven. Be satisfied in your suffering. I think that's terrible. Let me say that to a great extent the church has been paternalistic toward poor people. The soup line, clothing the poor, has always been the satisfaction of the rich in condescending toward the poor. The theology of liberation just blows that out. I think the Catholic Church, of all other churches, is going to have a harder time because it is so built that any change has to come from Rome to the bishops to the parish. It is hard to break through that. Some of the priests are having a hard time in dealing with parish councils because the parishioners are *vivos* (intelligent) and not settling for double standards.

GUERRERO: It isn't liberating itself.

ANGUIANO: Oh, no, it isn't. I think that's only going to happen when there are not enough clergy to go around, and the lay people assume the position of priests.

GUERRERO: When they assume the position of being priests and start running the parishes then we are really going to see a change in the hierarchy of the church.

•

RUBÉN ARMENDARIZ: Theology would teach us that there is a danger in working from absolutes or in working from propositions or axioms that are unrelated to the reality of people. When you are able to work with propositions and axioms you can establish a sense of superiority; but if you begin with the *praxis*, with the level of the people, then you begin to reflect from your own circumstance. If you can make the proposition that God is love and say that it is a theological axiom, then those who are in power can say, "Well, the reason we are in power is because we love God and God loves us and that way we can do whatever we desire." Whereas if you look at a situation from the experience of the oppressed, you raise the question, "Okay, so God is love. How is God love? Where do we see God's love manifested?" Then we begin to raise all kinds of questions. I am not necessarily justified in doing whatever I want to because God loves me; rather I must ask what is my responsibility in that love of God. It's a challenge that comes from that love of God. It's a totally different perspective.

I do not believe that the established doctrines that have been proposed to us as axiomatic are necessarily relevant to us in the liberation process. I think we've come to a point where we have to say, as I would as a Presbyterian and taking for example the Westminster Confession, that God is infinite, eternal, omnipotent, and omnipresent. The minute I start to think about these things I say all of them are the things that I am not. That's deducing. It's a deduction method of saying who God is. But if I begin where I am and I raise questions—Why do my people suffer? What kind of God is this? That is a totally different perspective.

The founding of the United States in some ways took on the perspective of the axiomatic. There are many sermons to this effect. Robert Bellah, for example, in his book *The Broken Covenant* gives a great theological outlook in that people who were coming over looked at the United States as the New Jerusalem. They were leaving the Old Babylon. They were the promised people and God in his sovereign right had decreed that they should own all this. It is part of the Manifest Destiny. That concept operates out of axiomatic propositions.

I don't think that we as Hispanics in the liberation process can afford that. When we say that God is love, I think we are raising a question, and it is not an axiomatic proposition. It is a question. God is love. What follows from that is: How do we see God? How is God eternal? How is God infinite? How is God omnipresent?

How do we acknowledge God through our own actions?

GUERRERO: I remember we were always told who we were as Christians but we were never told how to be Christians.

ARMENDARIZ: That's right, and that is because it comes from an axiomatic proposition: You are a Christian. The question "how" is a practical one. It begins here where you live.

GUERRERO: Küng's book *On Being a Christian* asks, but it doesn't really teach, how to be a Christian. I think that European theology has never left the realm of the dominant. Liberation theology goes into the realm of the oppressed. It takes a leap of faith.

ARMENDARIZ: Liberation theology says, "Look, that is irrelevant because it does not really speak to your concrete situation of oppression. You have to start here."

"Let my people go, so that they may keep a feast in the wilderness in honor of me" (Ex 5:1–2)

In Latin American, Black, and African liberation theologies I found that the Exodus theme was constantly stressed. My interest was to find out what our Chicano leaders thought about this theme. The shared theme was stated as follows:

Black theology, African theology, and Latin American libera-
tion theology have used the theme of Exodus from the Old
Testament as a biblical starting point. In Exodus, against
much opposition from Pharaoh, Moses led the Hebrews out
of Egypt. Without God's help Moses would not have suc-
ceeded. What are your thoughts on the Exodus event in the
Old Testament as compared to the Chicano cosmic experi-
ence of oppression? Is the Exodus theme a viable theme for a
Chicano theology of liberation?

RICARDO SÁNCHEZ: Only if we were invading somebody else's land. We are in our own land. Instead of Exodus another Judaic concept is more appropriate to our human and social condition, and that is the concept of the diaspora. It is not a question of our leaving Atzlán.[12] We've been wandering all over Atzlán without feeling that we are part of Atzlán. At some point, economically, politically, philosophically, from every perspective we can talk about in terms of being human beings, we must reclaim our land. We must not reclaim it to be the masters of it, to be the dominant force, but to participate in a meaningful, humanistic, wholistic manner with all that exists within what is now our land. For we do not even have a voice in any sense of the word.

What has relevance to me is not let my people go, but rather my people must get their sovereignty as a people. We must determine that somehow we can live here, because we are the only people, here together with the American Indian, who continue surviving within the United States as an autonomous people under treaty. We did not come here. We were not brought here; we are the land, the skies, and the rivers. It is not a question of letting us go. Stop imperialistically enslaving us as a people, either individually or collectively. Respect those laws, the Treaty of Guadalupe-Hidalgo or whatever, adhere to them for the first time. Adhere to those parchments, documents that talk about the equality of human beings; adhere to them for the first time, *Norte Amerika*. Begin to think of keeping one of your promises, not just a promise to take the land and exploit the inhabitants of the land, but the promise that's allegedly so inherent in those documents as written by the elitist framers of the Constitution and the Declaration of Independence. I say elitist because they were landowners who framed those documents, and reading through the lines you get the feeling that perhaps what they meant was that only those who had land were equal; the other ones weren't—the indentured, the Indian, the culturally different and the religiously different. It is only through much travail and struggle that people have begun to have a semblance of rights, on paper of course, but not in practical reality.

Let my people go, in a sense, yes, that is apropos because we are slaves; there can be no denying that. Not only are Chicanos slaves, Blacks are slaves, and Indians are slaves, but poor whites are slaves *también*. The suffering of the Appalachian poor is no different than the suffering of the Chicano poor, no different than the suffering of the Black poor, the Indian poor in the reservations who commit suicide at fourteen because life is so horrible, so rancid— not life, the thing that forces through our minds or bodies or souls, not life that way, but societal life, society itself with its privileges for the few at the expense of the many.

Perhaps it is not so much "let my people go" that is important but rather to end that type of imperialism that negates us as human beings. I go back to the idea of the diaspora in our own land. We wander from south Texas up to Michigan, to California, all over the country. Wandering as migrants to produce the food that will feed the wealthy, while the migrant farm worker, who in the main is Chicano, suffers from malnutrition, goes to bed hungry every night. His children have distended stomachs, swollen eyes, hurt, deprivation, vitamin deficiency, rickets, so many different things that are endemic to our people. We have more polio cases in Texas than in the rest of the entire nation. And those polio cases came out of the winter gardens in the Rio Grande Valley, and they are Chicano. Why? Because vaccine is not available for the poor in this part of the country. We have plague and pest and what-not in the barrio. We have so many different illnesses that do not exist in the rest of the westernized industrialized states of the world, but they do exist in the Chicano community.

The poorest cities historically have been the bastions of the Chicano—San Antonio, Corpus Christi, El Paso, Laredo, Brownsville; the five poorest cities per capita in the United States are places where we predominate. And not because we are destined to be poor, but because we have been kept from all those things that will facilitate or engender growth, progressiveness, well-being.

Yes, it's more than let us go. Perhaps it is White America, those who rule—I'm not talking about the average white persons, even though they may have a $75,000 mortgage on their house and a $4,000 to $10,000 mortgage on their car. They are enslaved; they're in park. They can't do anything but continue in the same rut, going round and round in a circle, getting nowhere. Not those, those are not the ones who are the enemies. Those are also frustrated human beings, middle class, but also hurting.

No, the enemies are people with the real power, who dictate policies that are serving their own needs. I'm talking about those people who influence the world. Those people should be the ones to become more humanizing, more ultimately human beings in concern and caring love.

Yes, they do have programs against us. There is genocide. Chicanos suffer the same kind of genocide that Jews have through our

Indian reality, through our *mestizo* reality, through the destruction of our language, through the destruction of our culture, and through the imposition that tells us if we want to survive here we must assimilate! The only model we have is that stuffy linear model that says nothing to us about our spirituality.

Our churches condone it. They haven't done any better. They work hand in hand with the growers; they work hand in hand with the industrialists; they work hand in hand with the prison wardens to destroy us, to pillory us in every way they can. Yes, we see it in many ways. We are abused, misused; we are killed.

It's not just let my people go; it is also stop murdering our people, stop murdering our ideas, our hopes, our needs. Stop murdering the need that all human beings have to respect themselves, existentially, philosophically, spiritually.

The cry, the plea of our people, all the peoples in this continent has been: "Yes, let us be free. Once, someday, let us taste of it." Not the freedom to go and kill in Vietnam or any other uprising. Not the new crusade against the new infidels, wherever they may be, for social, economic, and political aggrandizement, but the cries for peace, serenity, and a means to luxuriate in thinking, in creativity, in realizing that your children will eat food that will nurture their bodies, and that they will have access to materials that will nurture their minds and their souls. Their reflection will be manifested throughout the social fabric, not as furtive, isolated, alienated beings who can put tatoos on their hands, arms, backs, and who will put graffiti on the wall trying to say, "I too exist: I think; therefore I am." The reason I know that I think and that I am is because I can indicate it. I can write it somewhere, if only on my body or on a wall in a decaying tenement building in a barrio in El Paso, in Los Angeles, in San Antonio, in Albuquerque. I have no other means of expressing my humanity because I have been kept voiceless.

Or perhaps it is a new Exodus, a new intellectual spiritual Exodus wherein people begin to reaffirm and manifest their humanity by being able to create. To create is to have the means to create, not the mind, because we all have the mind. We are capable of writing fine poetry, of creating beautiful music and painting fantastic pictures and becoming tremendous architects, but lack the access to do it. We need to be able to get into that process where the resources reside so that we can have the means of owning and of truly developing our talents and our minds.

That is the Exodus, the coming-out of these enclaves of poverty, destitution, and denigration into that world where our minds have value, where our spirituality can manifest itself, where we can walk beautifully and proudly. Then we won't have to just survive; we can thrive, all human beings can thrive. That kind of an Exodus, an Exodus out of poverty, horror, and fear, and pestilence, and ignorance and lack of education, medical treatment, and so many different things. And realizing that medical treatment, a good education, good food, and all those things are human rights— human rights—because the world belongs to all the people of the world, not to the few who can manipulate, but to all the people of the world.

No, it's more than let my people go. Let us go into that world that is also ours, this land. Let us go into it in every way we can to create something we must create.

It is not a question only of the master allowing. It's a question of doing it, in spite of the fact that some people stand there to be masters. It's a question of our no longer being slaves, or remaining cool, no longer being followers but creators because we have it within us as human beings to create a new way of life. It's a question of our saying that we truly love ourselves, that we truly love our children who are given examples of courage, not acquiescence. No more, "*Sí, patrón.*" Nobody was born with an inherent right to be a *patrón*! Nobody was born with an inherent responsibility to be a willing slave. Those who are in master positions enforce the system by being despoilers of human life, desecrators in the finest sense of the word. They desecrate all that is humane and plausible. That's how I see it.

•

RUBÉN ARMENDARIZ: I've given a lot of thought to that. At first I was intrigued by the Exodus theme in that it contains the whole imagery of slavery, exploitation, abused marginal people within a particular society. Then I began to think that if we use the Exodus theme we are really negating our historical reality. If you remember, the War of 1848 really was a way of appropriating our people. If one uses the Exodus theme, then one admits that one is a stranger in another land.

Moses came to liberate the people from the land of Egypt, to take them to a promised land. If you are talking about the Chicano, you're talking about the whole Southwest. You're dealing with a piece of real estate that was taken during the Manifest Destiny period from Mexico where we already belonged. So I find a difficulty in using the Exodus theme to speak about letting my people go. There is some very good imagery there in that people are held in captivity, people are held against their will, people are not allowed to practice their own religious understanding and culture. Yet, there are some limitations to this theme. I've wrestled with this a great deal. Is it proper for us to use that theme, let my people go? Or is it better to speak only in terms of captivity, because we are held captive in our land? See, I think there is a danger in using that imagery and applying it here.

The war with Mexico was fought, and we became citizens because of an acquisition. Therefore, it seems to me there is a problem there. How do we resolve it? How do we speak about liberation in terms of land? I'm not sure. I haven't come up with the answer except to say that we must be very careful that we do not forget that we were here first.

CONCLUSION

By utilizing the "shared theme" method to acquire the oral tradition material, I discovered that Chicanos did have much in common. The method proved valuable: I acquired data, and the interviewees were able to express themselves.

All the interviewees agreed that Chicanos are oppressed and need to concentrate on various aspects of liberation. Liberation was not only physical, but also psychological and spiritual. Six opted for nonviolence as a necessary option for liberation. Three opted for any means necessary to acquire liberation.

Almost all agreed that the church was not doing all it was capable of doing for Chicanos and other Hispanic groups. Yet there was also the feeling that the church was the last hope for Chicanos in the Southwest. Through programs sponsored by the church, one interviewee suggested, the tradition, identity, culture, and language of the Chicano could be preserved. Almost all agreed that today's European white theology leaves out the perspective of the oppressed. Chicanos need a theology of liberation of their own to relate to their experience and needs.

The question of the land is an open question. Chicanos have a strong affinity with the land. Education does not necessarily imply a better response to or greater sympathy with the oppression of Chicanos. Education usually means assimilation into the dominant culture. Chicano males still need to work in overcoming the *machismo* myth. The issue of race takes precedence over the issue of class. The lighter Chicanos have better opportunities than the darker ones.

Fatalism and anarchism are not necessarily negative characteristics. There are some positive cultural attributes attached to both of these phenomena. Chicanos do relate to the impoverished of the world and their needs, especially in Latin America.

Chicanos with their *corazón latino* and gringo impulse are a hope for the hemisphere and a bridge between the rich and poor nations. A Chicano theology of liberation must take into account the Chicano oral tradition in order to speak to Chicano needs and to find avenues of expressing Chicano potential and capability.

CHAPTER 4

The Religious Symbol of Guadalupe

A BRIEF HISTORY OF GUADALUPE

In 1660 the Catholic Church officially declared that Our Lady of Guadalupe is the Blessed Virgin Mary.[1] In 1754 Pope Benedict XIV said of Mexico, *Non fecit taliter omni nationi* ("God has not done likewise with any other nation").[2] "We declare, decree and command that the Mother of God called Our Lady of Guadalupe be recognized, invoked and venerated as Patroness and Protectress of Mexico."[3]

To understand the symbol of Guadalupe is to understand the essence of being Mexican. Traditionally this essence has carried over to the Chicanos in the American Southwest, where the symbol of Guadalupe exists vividly. Almost every Chicano city has a church named after Guadalupe. A major river in Texas is named the Guadalupe River. Many Chicanos, both male and female, bear her name. Guadalupe, like Jesus, is very real to us. We are constantly reminded of her presence by the names of our relatives and friends.

Nuestra Señora de Guadalupe appeared to Juan Diego, an Aztec, on December 9, 1531. Every Saturday after his and his wife's baptism, Juan would pass by the hill of Tepeyac as he walked the two miles from Tolpetlac to Tlatelolco to hear Our Blessed Lady's Mass sung at dawn. One morning he heard music coming from the top of the hill. As he approached to investigate, a young woman, an Aztec maiden, appeared to him. She asked that a temple be built in her honor. She also said: "I will give all my love and motherly compassion to those who seek my aid."[4]

Our Lady of Guadalupe appeared to Juan Diego three more times and to his uncle, Juan Bernardino, once.[5] The first three times Juan Diego was not believed by Fray Juan Zumárraga, the first bishop of Mexico. Bishop Zumárraga told Juan to ask the Virgin to give him a sign. The sign she gave was her image imprinted on Juan Diego's *tilma*,[6] which the Virgin instructed Juan to fill with roses. The image is now displayed in the Basilica of Guadalupe in Mexico City.

Controversy exists as to the proper name of Guadalupe. Some people believe that she was named after a virgin of Guadalupe who already existed in a monastery in Estremadura, Spain. Besides this controversial theory there are others. The following one has a strong tradition.

Juan Bernardino, the uncle of Juan Diego, was terminally ill at the time of the fourth apparition. Because of his uncle's illness Juan Diego had not taken his usual route at the foot of the hill of Tepeyac. He took a different route to get help for his uncle. Guadalupe appeared to him for the last time. Juan Diego told her why he had avoided her. She told Juan Diego not to worry about his uncle and that he would recover. When the Virgin appeared to Juan Bernardino and he asked her name, she answered that she was the Immaculate Virgin, Holy Mary of Guadalupe.[7] The Virgin spoke to Juan Bernardino in the Nahuatl language, as she had to Juan Diego. Instead of *Guadalupe* Juan Bernardino could have heard the Virgin say *Coatlaxopeuh*, which in Nahuatl is pronounced *cuatlashupe*.[8] "*Coatl* stands for serpent, *tla* is an expletive particle, and *xopeuh* means crushed or stepped on with disdain."[9]

This concept would have had meaning to the native Americans because it was at Tepeyac that a temple for Teotenantzín, mother of God, existed before the coming of the Spaniards. If we follow this theory of *Coatlaxopeuh*, we would read "the Holy Virgin Mary who crushed the serpent." The serpent was symbolic of the old Aztec religion, which annually required the sacrifice of thousands of human lives. The Virgin's new religion would take the place of the old Aztec religion. Guadalupe was such a strong symbol for the native Americans (not even the Spaniards understood how strong) because she appeared at Tepeyac. During the seven years after her apparition eight million native Americans were baptized into the

Catholic faith.[10] Since then Guadalupe has never lost her symbolic strength among Mexicans and Chicanos. The strength of the symbol is exemplified in the following analysis of several of the translated verses of songs sung in honor of Guadalupe by Mexicans and Chicanos.

AN ANALYSIS OF SELECTED VERSES OF SONGS FROM THE LITURGICAL MASS OF GUADALUPE

In *Propios de la misa de Nuestra Señora de Guadalupe* five religious songs are dedicated to her honor. What we find in those verses is more than just an admiration for Guadalupe. The Mexican and Chicano people love and identify with Guadalupe. The phenomenon is of such strength that I believe that without Guadalupe there would be no Mexico—and without Mexico there would be no Guadalupe. For Mexicans and Chicanos, Guadalupe is not a companion, a wife, sister, or daughter. She is a mother. It is important to grasp this concept in order to understand her symbolic role.

Desde el cielo una hermosa mañana

Desde el cielo una hermosa mañana

From the heavens one beautiful morning

La Guadalupana bajó al Tepeyac.

Guadalupe descended to Tepeyac.

Suplicante juntaba las manos
y eran Mexicanas su porte y su faz.

Humbly, she joined her hands
and they were Mexican, her expression and her face.

Su llegada llenó de alegría
de luz y armonía
todo el Anahuac.

Her arrival filled with joy,
happiness, and harmony
all the valley of Mexico.

Junto al monte pasaba Juan Diego
y acércase luego al oír cantar:

Near the hill passed Juan Diego
and coming closer he heard her singing:

*"Juan Dieguito," la Virgen
    le dijo,
"este cerro elijo para hacer
    mi altar."*

"Juan Dieguito," the Virgin
    told him,
"I have chosen this hill to
    have my altar built."

*Y en la tilma entre rosas pin-
    tadas
su imagen amada se dignó
    dejar.*

And in the *tilma* among
    beautiful roses
She left her beloved image.

*Desde entonces para el Me-
    xicano
ser Guadalupano es algo
    esencial.*

Since then for the Mexican,
To be a Guadalupano is es-
    sential.

*Madrecita de los Mexicanos
Que estás en el cielo
Ruega a Dios por nos.*

Beloved Mother of all Mexi-
    cans
You who are in heaven
Pray to God for us.

This song recounts the story of the apparition, the Virgin's request, and her identity. Verse 2 shows that she is without any doubt Mexican. Not only is her physical appearance Mexican, but also her mannerisms, her ways, *sus modos*. Verse 3 is important to the survival of the native Americans because after the Spanish conquest, they experienced nothing but suffering, despair, and degradation. Her arrival symbolized the hope that was necessary for them to survive. Verse 7 is the climactic conclusion: to be Mexican is to be a Guadalupano.

The apparition not only insured the survival of the native American; it sealed their allegiance to Guadalupe. Verse 8 emphasizes Guadalupe's role as beloved mother of all Mexicans, including the Chicanos in the Southwest. Guadalupe was and continues to be the mother of the oppressed native Americans and *mestizos* in Mexico and in the Chicano Southwest.

Mañanitas a la Virgen

*Oh Virgen la mas hermosa
del valle del Anahuac,*

O Virgin most beautiful
of the valley of Mexico,

tus hijos muy de mañana
te vienen a saludar.

your children very early in
 the morning
come to greet you.

Coro
Despierta, madre, despierta,
mira que ya amaneció.
Ya los pajaritos cantan,
la luna ya se metió.

Chorus
Wake up, mother, wake up.
See, it's already morning.
The birds are already sing-
 ing
and the moon has set.

Aquella alegre mañana
en que apareciste a Juan
 mientras
Dios me dé la vida,
nunca se me olvidará.

That joyous morning
in which you appeared to
 Juan,
as long as God gives me life
I will never forget it.

Cuando miro tu carita
llena de tanto candor,
Quisiera darte mil besos
para mostrarte mi amor.

When I see your lovely face
full of such kindness,
I wish I could give you a
 thousand kisses,
to show you my love.

Madre de los Mexicanos
dijiste venías a ser.
Pues ya lo ves, morenita,
Sí te sabemos querer.

Mother of all Mexicans
you said you had come to
 be.
Well, you can see, *morenita*,
We do know how to love
 you.

Verses 3, 4, and 5 all tell of our admiration and love for Guadalupe.

Viva la Virgen de Guadalupe

Viva la Virgen de Guada-
 lupe,
que en nuestro pecho tiene
 un altar.

Long live the Virgin of
 Guadalupe,
who in our bosom has her
 altar.

Y reine siempre triumfante Cristo	And may our Christ always triumph
en nuestro pueblo noble y leal.	in our country noble and faithful.
Siempre seremos tus fieles hijos.	We will always be your faithful children.
Nuestra abogada siempre serás.	Our mediatrix you will always be.
Y con tu ayuda perpetua siempre derrotaremos a Satanás.	And with your perpetual help we will defeat Satan.
Siempre seremos tus fieles hijos.	We will always be your faithful children.
Nuestro Rey siempre será Jesús,	Our King will always be Jesus,
Hoy te lo juran los hombres todos	Today all people swear it to you
arrodillados ante la Cruz.	kneeling before the cross.

The three verses of this song bring out the patriotism and loyalty of the Mexican people to Guadalupe. Also to be found is a profound faithfulness to her as the Mother of Jesus Christ, whom Catholic Mexicans and Chicanos accept as their savior and king.

O Virgen de Guadalupe

O Virgen de Guadalupe	O Virgin of Guadalupe,
Yo te vengo a saludar	I have come to say hello
Y a traerte mi cariño	And to bring my love
hasta el trono de tu altar.	to the throne of your altar.
Este día en que mostraste	This day in which you demonstrate
tu cariño maternal,	your maternal love,
nuestro humildes canciones	Mother, you deign
dígnate medio eschuchar.	to listen to our humble songs.

Hoy a tus pies acudimos	Today, Mother, you look
dígnate, madre, mirar,	down upon us
a estos tus hijos que	who run to your feet,
amantes,	To these your children, who,
se postran ante tu altar.	loving you,
	kneel before your altar.
Eres virgen toda pura	You are a virgin all pure
de hermosura sin igual,	of beauty without equal,
y aplastaste la cabeza	and you crushed the head
de la serpiente infernal.	of the infernal serpent.
Hoy en el día en que veniste	Today, the day on which you
nuestro suelo a visitar,	came
venimos agradecerte tu	to visit our humble soil,
cariño maternal.	We come to express our
	gratitude
	for your maternal love.

This song expresses the love that Mexicans and Chicanos have for Guadalupe. Gratitude for her motherly love is also expressed. In verse 4 we see that it is she who crushes the serpent's head. This symbolism is important in understanding the dual role of Guadalupe. Not only is she a loving mother but she crushes the symbol of evil (sin) in Christian thought. This could easily be interpreted as defeating those evil forces that create oppression; hence her title *"libertadora de las razas oprimidas."*[11]

La Virgen Ranchera

A tí, Virgencita,	To you, dear Virgin,
Mi Guadalupana,	My Guadalupana,
Ya quiero ofrecerte	I want to offer you
un canto valiente	a courageous song
Que México entero	Which all Mexico sings
Te diga sonriente.	to you with joy.
Y quiero decirte lo que tu ya	And I want to tell you
sabes	what you already know,
que México te ama,	that Mexico loves you,

que nunca está triste,
porque de nombrarte
El alma se inflama.

that it is never sad,
because on proclaiming
    your name
the soul catches fire.

Todos
Tu nombre es arrullo
y el mundo lo sabe,
Eres nuestro orgullo,
mi México es tuyo.
Tu guardas las llaves.

All
Your name is a lullaby
and the world knows it.
You are our pride,
my Mexico is yours.
You guard the keys.

Que viva la Reina
de los Mexicanos
la que con sus manos
sembró rosas bellas
y puso en el cielo
Millares de estrellas.

Long live the Queen
of the Mexicans,
the one whose hands
planted beautiful roses
and put in the heavens
thousands of stars.

Ya sé que en el cielo
tu eschuchas mi canto,
y sé que con celo
nos cubre tu manto.
Virgencita chula,
Eres un encanto.

I know that in heaven
you listen to my songs,
and I know that jealously
your veil covers us.
Lovely Virgin,
you are an enchantment.

Por patria nos diste,
este lindo suelo
y lo bendlijiste
porque era tu anhelo
tener un santuario
cerquita del cielo

For a nation you gave us
this beautiful land,
and you blessed it
because it was your desire
to have a sanctuary
closer to heaven.

Todos
Mi Virgen Morena,
Mi Virgen Ranchera,
Eres nuestra Reina,
México es tu tierra
Y tu su bandera.

All
My Brown Virgin,
My *Ranchera* Virgin,
You are our Queen,
Mexico is your land,
And you are its flag.

Que viva la Reina	Long live the Queen
de los Mexicanos	of the Mexicans,
la que con sus manos	the one whose hands
sembró rosas bellas	planted beautiful roses
y puso en el cielo	and put in the heavens
Millones de estrellas.	millions of stars.

From these verses we can see that Guadalupe plays a major role in Mexican nationalism. As queen of Mexico she is more than a strong psychological-social phenomenon. When Chicanos use the expression *mi reina*, they mean something very cordial, very special, very warm, very affectionate.

Verse 6 brings out the brown identity of Guadalupe and the *ranchera* identity. *Ranchero* is more a *mestizo* reality than a native American reality. In *ranchos* (ranches) the rural *mestizos* and native Americans work for the *patrones* (bosses). Calling Guadalupe *ranchera morena* (brown) identifies her with the masses of Mexico's poor working class. In the rural Southwest this concept of Guadalupe as *ranchera* is very vivid for Chicanos. In the urban Southwest the concept of *ranchera* serves to retain the folklore and tradition of the rural Chicanos. It symbolizes the strong relationship Chicanos had with the country, field, farm, and ranch life before they moved to the city.

ANALYZING THE THEME OF *NUESTRA SEÑORA DE GUADALUPE* FROM THE ORAL TRADITION

I presented the shared theme as follows:

Almost all Chicano Catholic homes in the barrios of the Southwest display Guadalupe's picture. Pachucos sometimes tattoo her entire image on their backs. In the context of the Chicano experience of oppression Guadalupe is a strong symbolic spiritual mother who is always there to lend a helping hand to the poor. Moreover, because of our oppression, we Chicanos strongly identify our experience and the Suffering Christ. One has only to look at the gruesome crucifixes in our Chicano churches to deduce that Christ is one of us. Hence, the concept of Guadalupe as a liberator and

*a mother of the oppressed is very real to us. Miguel Hidalgo
de Costilla, Emiliano Zapata, and César Chávez have all
symbolically advocated her assistance in warding off institutions of government and capital interests that breed oppression. What are your thoughts on Guadalupe as she relates to
the Chicano cosmic experience of oppression?*

Of all the symbols that Guadalupe represented to the Chicano
leaders I interviewed, the following were the ones I chose to present
here: Guadalupe as a symbol of faith, as a symbol of identity, as a
symbol of hope, as a symbol of woman against *machismo*, and as a
symbol of liberation.

Guadalupe as a Symbol of Faith

Of the nine Chicano leaders that I interviewed it was the two
women, Dolores Huerta and Lupe Anguiano, who saw La Virgen
de Guadalupe as a symbol of faith. Faith is that mystery in us that
drives us to believe in something we cherish and hold dearly but do
not see. We cannot prove the existence of God or that Jesus Christ is
the Son of God. We have faith as Christians that God exists, and we
believe that Jesus Christ is God's only begotten Son. We also trust
that these articles of faith are true because we have been taught that
they are so by our elders, by the tradition of the church, and by our
parents who are part of a larger believing community. So the
element of trusting in something or someone is included in our
understanding of faith. We trust that we are not being deceived.
The truth handed down to the Mexican nation was that the miraculous apparition was a revelation.

Guadalupe appeared as an Aztec maiden. No Indian doubted
that she was Indian. Moreover, she appeared to an Indian, one of
the downtrodden, not to a Spaniard. We could say that, politically,
she appeared on the side of the oppressed. When I asked Dolores
Huerta, "What about the fact that Chávez uses her when he makes
his marches?" Dolores responded:

She is a symbol of the impossible, of doing the impossible to
win a victory, in humility, of being able to win with the faith. I
mean that's the important thing that she symbolizes to the

union: that with faith you can win. You know with faith you can overcome. She is a symbol of faith, of the miraculous. We always celebrate *el día de la Virgen*. . . . In our strikes, we always have the Virgin with us. That's important *palanca* [moral support].

When *campesinos* like the Farm Workers strike against the growers and against agribusinesses that have economic and political connections in the State Houses and in the federal government, it takes almost a miracle to win. It is like David fighting Goliath. The *campesinos* are impoverished. They have no money, no political connections, no influence in power positions. Most Chicanos are Catholic. When Dolores and César began their strikes in California, it was not the Catholic Church that came to their assistance first. It was the Anglo Protestant Church. But even though in the beginning the Catholic Church as an institution did not support them, Nuestra Señora de Guadalupe was with them.

Msgr. Longinus Reyes said:

Se los tragó el sistema.[12] This is what has happened to La Guadalupana. We're not hearing her *mensaje* (message). We're not sensing and feeling her love for the poor. We romanticize her. We don't really understand why she appeared to Juan Diego, who Juan Diego really was, and who the Juan Diego of today is, *el mestizo, el pobre*. Ironically though she is always there. Even though she is being used, the *pobre, el oprimido* always have her in front. Like you mentioned with Chávez, *las marchas*, and all these things. She is always there; she is a real live, strong symbol of *liberación. Es un proceso de concientización*.

Msgr. Reyes tells us that even though the church and the Chicanos misuse Guadalupe to legitimize the status quo (the way things are but not the way things ought to be), Guadalupe does not abandon or forget the poor. Her symbol is right there with them, in the forefront, waving and demonstrating to the world the cause of justice for oppressed Chicanos. In the Chicano experience, the mother is always there. The father may abandon the children, but it is rare for the mother to abandon them.

Chicanos believe that Guadalupe, our mother, loves the poor. They have her and they have faith that she will intercede for them because she stays with them. As long as she is around, they can depend on her. She will not abandon them.

Lupe Anguiano also said that Guadalupe was a symbol of faith for her. She presented the symbolic meaning a little differently. She said:

> To me she is a symbol of faith. She comes into our lives and shows us our importance as human beings and the love that God has for us. Many times I've asked myself what would I be, what would I do if I didn't have my faith, my faith in Christ, in God, my strong Christian belief, and I guess I came to the conclusion that I just wouldn't be. I just cannot imagine myself even intellectually comprehending the idea that I could exist without my faith. To me she is the symbol of introducing me to Christ. It is my guiding light. It is what I pull to.

Unlike Dolores's social conception of Guadalupe as a symbol of faith, Lupe journeys into the inner recesses of the Chicana's spirit. Lupe's symbol is a personal concept of faith. Without that "guiding light," without that sort of "pull to" faith in Christ, in God, and I might add in the church, things would be very difficult. For Chicanos faith in Christ is strengthened by our personal faith in Guadalupe. She enriches our faith with Christian values.

The Indian value systems are also intertwined with these Christian values. Through Guadalupe we not only retain aspects of our native American culture, we also adopt faith in Jesus Christ. We do not betray our own selves and we do not assimilate completely the European model of Christianity. So on the personal basis of faith we remain true to both our worlds as *mestizos*; we are Spanish and we are Indian.

Guadalupe as a Symbol of Identity

The two Chicano leaders interviewed who are traditionally Protestant developed the concept of Guadalupe as a symbol of identity more powerfully than did the Catholics. Catholics take her for granted. Protestants cannot take her for granted because for them the Virgin, the Mother of God, is a delicate issue. Theologically, Chicano Protestants cannot accept Guadalupe. This poses a problem for them because, like all Chicanos, culturally they are Guadalupanos.

Tomás Atencio, a Protestant sociologist, maintains that Chicanos are still very traditional. Modernization and secularization have not totally affected Chicano symbols and meaning structures. "The symbol remains in spite of modernized society breaking up." "Symbols are hard to kill because we are still traditional." Atencio went on:

> We believe that myth is basically energy. It is energy that is put together by human consciousness. So *la Virgen de Guadalupe* is a symbol that is rooted in myth. It is that same energy that created matter. But somehow it is put together so that it is meaningful. Values are the molecules of myth, beliefs, profound beliefs. Rather than instrumental values, I am talking about values that we call virtues. The arrangement of those virtues is what makes the myth. Within that myth we have certain symbols. The *Virgen de Guadalupe* is a very important symbol because it ties us to our Indian past. Its manifestation ties us to our traditional past.

Atencio maintains that the symbol of Guadalupe is the glue that keeps the structures together: the politics, the kinship system, the mutual aid societies, modern-day association groups, and the church as an institution. In this sense, the symbol is a very important element of our existence. We need Guadalupe not only spiritually, but also socially and politically. It gives us a basis for who we are and a sense of direction about where we are going. The symbol of Guadalupe weaves in and out of our spiritual, social, and political reality.

Atencio also spoke of the relationship of Guadalupe to the economic aspect of our reality. The tragedy of the economic is that as Chicanos become more middle class, they tend to forsake their belief system. Guadalupe, a symbol of the oppressed, could be wiped out by secularization and modernization. "Symbols can be killed or wiped out," Atencio says. Up to now this has not happened.

Even though people become very middle class, *pero todavía es Chicano* (they are still Chicano). You can't quite explain that because being Chicano is not demonstrated by a person's car or house, but rather by that person's belief system. That belief may not be practiced, but then when you get a movement going for resistance like in the Old Town, San Felipe, then it becomes very, very important.

Atencio says: "In the Chicano it is a folk Catholicism, a traditional Catholicism, that has a lot of faith in symbols, a lot of faith in myth and magic and those are the things that create the meaning structures for a people." So for Atencio, Guadalupe as a symbol of identity creates not only a meaningful structure of who we are, but also creates in us a meaningful structure of resistance against that which threatens that identity, whether it be political, cultural, religious, social, or economic.

Rubén Armendariz understands the role of Guadalupe as a symbol of a culture that identifies with the mother rather than with the father (as in the Judeo-Christian tradition). Armendariz tells us:

There is a consciousness that is already present in our make-up as Hispanics and even as Mexicans. As a Protestant, theologically, it would be heresy for me to admit to a Presbyterian that there is a value in promoting the understanding of the Virgin because historically that has been the contention. I find a very sad lack because the Hispanic has always identified primarily with the mother. I know for myself my father is a strong figure. He is an authority figure and so on. But when it comes to the real sentiment, when it comes to the feeling of the heart, when it comes to what I'm willing to die for, it's the mother. The worst blasphemy you can say is against my mother, not my father. You can say anything about my father. I am sure about my mother.

Armendariz has raised an interesting point: understanding Guadalupe as a symbol of identity is the essence of Chicano consciousness. Guadalupe as a symbol of identity forms a nucleus around which all the other phenomena of our culture revolve. The mother concept in the culture also serves as a nucleus. The woman concept plays a similar role. Armendariz said that when he was in the Navy what unified the Protestant and Catholic Chicanos was the Virgin of Guadalupe and their country (Mexico). Toward the end of the interview he repeated this statement and said: "In the service, when it came to the nitty-gritty it was for *la Virgen y mi madre.*" The unifying factor for the Chicanos as Armendariz experienced it in the Korean War was their consciousness of a symbol that all Chicanos had in common and with which all could culturally identify.

Armendariz maintains that the consciousness is deep-seated and precedes the apparition of the Virgin. His master's thesis (1961) was entitled *The Influence of Mariolatry in the Latin American Culture.* Perhaps it had to be a person who has been a Protestant all his life to write this thesis and to appreciate the symbol of Guadalupe as the essence of Chicano consciousness. The whole context of what the mother, the Virgin, the mother image in our culture means to us as oppressed persons is interwoven into this consciousness. In the Anglo culture the male image predominates. Theologically, Western Christianity has always dealt with God as Father.

Guadalupe as a Symbol of Hope

A general consensus among the Chicano leaders I interviewed was that the Catholic Church was possibly the only hope left for Chicanos in the Southwest. I feel Guadalupe plays a major symbolic role in that hope. José Ángel Gutiérrez tells us:

> One of the main criticisms that we have heard in the last two decades of this stage of the Chicano movement is that we lack an ideology. I have always quarreled with that statement because my view is that we suffer not from a lack of ideology but from the presence of many. The strongest ideology that we have is that founded in Christian principles rooted in Catholicism and manifested by symbols such as *la Virgen de Guadalupe.* Now the *Virgen de Guadalupe* in our case appeals both to our Indian heritage and to the European influence that we have from the Spaniards, so they get us from both sides of our culture with that symbol.

The last part of that quote is reminiscent of the point that Harvey Cox develops in his book *The Seduction of the Spirit*:

> I call the misuse of faith "the seduction of the spirit." Whether it is done by Churches or mass media, and whether individuals or groups are seduced, the process is pathetically the same: the seducer twists authentic inner impulses into instruments of domination.[13]

Cox goes on:

> The seduction of the spirit is a "religious" process. Both the individual and the group are led to depend on symbols laid upon them by their betters. But ironically, their defense against this fourflushery is also religious. In their inner spirits the victims know something is wrong and they continue, in furtive prayer, group memory and millennial fantasy, to be something other than what the dominating culture demands. . . . They nourish the hopes that one day they can win their full liberation, so they may celebrate openly what they must now remember in secret: "Let my people go that they might worship me."[14]

Both José Ángel Gutiérrez and Harvey Cox agree that religious symbols like Guadalupe are strong symbols of identity, which more often than not may be used against the people. At the same time embedded in those symbols is the hope for liberation in the future. But how is the hope embedded, unless, as Bishop Chávez says, "There has to be a process of liberation already going on in order for the symbol to be effective."

Guadalupe has been with Mexicans and Chicanos for four hundred and fifty years. She becomes an effective symbol when people, a leader, a prophet, can no longer tolerate injustices. *Cuando la opresión ya basta.*[15] Religious symbols such as Guadalupe reaffirm the hope in the people that there is a better way, that there is a limit to a people's suffering. The hope is always buried by forces beyond the poor people's capacity to overcome or even understand until the day of liberation. Hope is always there because with the new day of liberation new forces of oppression will be born. A new hope is then born, which will overcome the new forces of oppression. The symbols are the insurance of a people's purity of intention, of a people's vision of truth about who they are and where they are going.

Symbols can be the safeguards of what is good in the culture, and when they are that they do not die. Symbols are the mirrors that reflect a people's concept of reality, which may be distorted by human influences of domination or even by false concepts of reality that to the people at first seem to be real and positive but later turn out to be negative and sometimes even destructive. Symbols are the mysteries that unify a people in space and time. Destroy those symbols and you destroy the people. Kill these meaning structures and the people become assimilated or disenchanted, or give up and die.

> Breaking the pole meant the end of the cosmos, the return of chaos. Finally, they (as Chilpan) lay down upon the ground together and quietly waited for death.[16]

When people speak about spiritual conquests, broken poles, and the failure to return to their sacred cosmic centers, they are speaking about meaningful structures that no longer give them a reason to exist. The spiritual defeat is a physical defeat. In reference to Guadalupe, who else is a Guadalupano but a Mexicano or a Chicano? Now with many Catholic Mexicans and Chicanos converting to Protestantism, Guadalupe is pushed to the background theologically but not culturally. Culturally she is still there, unless one divorces oneself from the Mexican and Chicano culture and assimilates into the predominant Anglo-Saxon culture.

Ricardo Sánchez and Msgr. Longinus Reyes maintain that as a Chicano one is neither Anglo-Saxon nor Mexican but rather both. A cultural *mestizaje* has occurred with the Chicano. In his book *Indología*, Vasconcelos (see chapter 5) stated that a merger between the Anglo culture and the Latino culture was possible. Together with Sánchez and Reyes, I believe that for Chicanos the merger has already happened. But what has not occurred is the response from Anglo-Saxons to help develop this perspective. It would be foolish to believe that they have the intention of responding in this way. Chicanos have to wake up from their political, psychological, social, economic, and spiritual slumber. They have to take the bull by the horns and wrestle him down.

José Ángel Gutiérrez reminds us:

> We have abused that symbol. The *Virgen de Guadalupe* has found herself on our banners, flags, posters, political buttons, bumper stickers, and in our rhetoric. We have made her a political activist on our side. I suppose that in a way it's a self-defense mechanism because it seems that all the other saints and images are against us just by the way they look. They look like the oppressors: they are all blond and blue-eyed, including the baby Jesus that we see there in the nativity scene. She is the only one that looks like us. I guess the Negritos have San Martín de Porres. We have abused her because we all make her part of our parcel and our package. I think that the *Virgen de Guadalupe* offers hope. The miracle is attributed to her. The revelation to a peasant, to an *indio*, is affirmation that she belongs to us. She is one of us. She is one of our oppressed. In that sense I think we find an alliance with her.

José Ángel Gutiérrez is correct in his analysis. In spite of the use and misuse of Guadalupe, she still remains a strong symbol of hope for Chicanos, who seek some cosmic order to their oppressed universal condition. "We need some sense of cosmic order and our myths are one of its major sources."[17]

Guadalupe as a Symbol of Woman against *Machismo*

Dolores Huerta said: "She came in the form of an Indian woman, an Indian maiden; that has an awful lot of meaning, especially in terms of *machismo*." For Huerta, Guadalupe is important because she guarantees a place for womanhood.

Macho is a Spanish word. It is not an Indian word. It was the Spanish conquistador who violated the Indian woman. As for *La Malinche*, "the traitor," the name given to Doña Marina, the mistress of Cortés, Reies Tijerina reminds us that Doña Marina told her sisters and her people, "We will be conquered, but a new people will be born of us and the Spaniards." "She was able to

understand the reasons for the conquest and why her people had
such a miserable, poor experience." Tijerina says that for Doña
Marina something better had come out of all this. The question was
how to survive the trials and tribulations. Understood in this
context, *La Malinche* is not a traitor, but rather a heroine who tells
her people not to lose hope, but to have patience; we will survive.

But why is *La Malinche* a traitor, or rather a scapegoat, to the
Mexican *macho*, whereas the *Virgen de Guadalupe* is his queen?[18]
Octavio Paz tells us that Guadalupe is the Virgin Mother and *La
Malinche* is the raped mother.[19] For Mexicans and Chicanos both
are our mothers. One is our spiritual mother and the other is one
that has been violated.

Now it is logical and rather easy to side with a Virgin Mother
because there is no conflict, there is no challenge; she came to us
directly as God's messenger. But a mother that has been violated,
raped, is difficult to accept. Yet that is what the *macho* has to
contend with: the historical concept of a raped mother. The positive
logical conclusion is for the *macho* to come to her aid, to sympathize with her, to fight at her side so that she will not be victimized
again. Instead the *macho la maltrata, la golpea, la maldice, y la
niega*;[20] he says that it was her fault that she was violated. In other
words the *macho* victimizes the victim further, his mother, his wife,
the woman. Thus we are the "*hijos de la chingada,*" the sons of the
Violated One.[21]

Underneath all this lies a deeper truth. We are "*hijos de la
chingada*" in the abstract, in the indeterminate, in the idea, in the
beyond. But in actuality, because we do not defend her, because we
do not fight, we males are cowards. On account of historical fear
(*la Conquista*), of economic fear (poverty and misery), of social
fear (what will the neighbors say), of political fear (we do not
organize ourselves), of psychological fear (our inferiority complex), of spiritual fear (let us find refuge in the Virgin of Guadalupe), we refuse to act and stand up for what is right and just. These
haunting fears restrict our destiny to fight.

Chicanos lose these fears when they realize that enough is
enough. So many centuries of being victimized in our own land
ought to enlighten us to have courage, to fight the masters for our
right to be. When the *macho* fights against Chicanas, he fights
against himself. He victimizes himself because she is also oppressed

as he is. The woman he loves cannot be the scapegoat of his jealousy, his fears, his terror of the gringo who victimizes them. Fear and terror is fought with the desire to be a human being. Human beings must fight out of their situation of oppression. Unjust circumstances force them to become liberators.

When the *macho* realizes that the Chicana is not his scapegoat and that Our Lady of Guadalupe, a symbol of our mother, is against *machismo*, then we will begin to appreciate what Dolores Huerta said about Mexicans and Chicanos being a special people. "Mexico is the only nation she has appeared to in this continent. It makes the Mexicanos/Chicanos a very special people because she appeared to them."

Guadalupe as a Symbol of Liberation

GUERRERO: You say they will lead us; could these symbols lead us?

SÁNCHEZ: No! If we redefine them, yes, but they wouldn't be leading us; we would be leading ourselves. It is not a question of our being led. I'm fighting the pretension that they lead us anywhere.

Ricardo Sánchez here states that if we lead ourselves out of a situation of oppression we redefine the models. Why does he say "if we redefine them"? How is Guadalupe defined anyway? Who defined or defines Guadalupe? I contend that she is defined differently by different interest groups. The church defines her one way; the *indio* defines her another; the Mexican and the Chicano define her still another way.

GUERRERO: They did us in with symbols?

SÁNCHEZ: Of course. And we accepted them in many ways. We had to; we had to survive.

Historically, with a few exceptions, the symbol of Guadalupe has not been proclaimed as a liberating symbol. When we see the situation of Chicanos and Indians today, again with few exceptions, Guadalupe is not liberating: The overall analysis of Sánchez is correct. The church as an institution, in more cases than one, for more reasons than one, has sided with the oppressor and has used Guadalupe to placate the Indians and the Chicanos. I do not think anyone would question that point. So how do we redefine Guadalupe as a symbol of liberation as opposed to a symbol of placation and passivity?

The symbol as such is not a liberating symbol, but it can be redefined as liberating provided that the people realize the process of liberation going on. As Sánchez says, "We lead ourselves, the symbol of Guadalupe does not lead us." We use the symbol in the process toward liberation. We use the symbol to give credence to our struggle. She is the symbol of faith. She is the symbol of hope. Now she is used as a symbol of our struggle for liberation.

Rubén Armendariz stated that Guadalupe was an expression of our religiosity and an expression of our nationality. As such she will be out in the forefront with the people. Both our religious character (what we believe in) and our national character (who we are politically) take on a new revelation, a new meaning in our existence. With Hidalgo the symbol of Guadalupe represented the Mexican coming to grips with independence. With Zapata she represented the Mexican grappling with a revolution for justice. With Chávez she represents the Chicano fighting the exploitation of farm workers by growers and agribusiness in terms of the Chicano's economic margin of existence in the United States.

What is Guadalupe saying to Chicanos about their church, which has no Chicano leadership? What is Guadalupe saying in terms of the educational deficiencies of Chicano children in the Southwest? What is she saying in terms of Texas Chicano children having a health record worse than any other children in the other forty-nine states?

How is her message being translated in terms of many of our leaders who do speak out and who defend the poor and who suddenly find themselves without jobs, without support from the church, and without support from the status quo community? How is her message being translated when Chicanos who run for office are literally destroyed by gringo political machines in Texas, New Mexico, Arizona, Colorado, and California? How is her message translated in terms of Chicanos selling out their own people by buying into political machines that exploit and gerrymander districts for selfish interests? How is Guadalupe translated in terms of materialistic capitalism? In terms of democratic socialism? In terms of human rights issues? In terms of world solidarity? How is Guadalupe translated in terms of the economic margins of existence that Chicanos share with Blacks, native Americans, poor white Americans, Africans, Asians, and Latin Americans? Guadalupe is translated according to the way all these questions address the poor (see chapter 6 for a discussion of the poor). Guadalupe as a symbol of liberation is the Mother of the Oppressed. Like any mother, she does not abandon her children nor does she fail to respond to their cries.

CONCLUSION

The phenomenon of Guadalupe is very real to Chicanos. By understanding Guadalupe, you understand Chicanos. In her poetry and songs one will find the history, the beauty, the spiritual role that the symbol of Guadalupe plays in the lives of Mexicans and Chicanos. As a symbol of faith she strengthens our belief in Jesus Christ; as a symbol of identity she is the essence of Chicano consciousness; as a symbol of hope she aids in our struggle to survive; as a symbol of the woman against *machismo* she beckons the *macho* to struggle at the side of women against oppression; as a symbol of liberation, in spite of her misuse by those in power, she is beside the poor as they fight oppression.

For Chicanos Guadalupe is opening up other areas of consciousness because of our identity with her: the role of women in our culture (which manifests *machismo*), the theological preoccupation with God the Mother, the ordination of women, the equality of women in Western Catholic culture, and (being children of the Guadalupana) the cosmic global unity with the oppressed.

GUERRERO: It gives Guadalupe a cosmic dimension.

ATENCIO: Yes, that is where your cosmic dimension comes in and the symbols are going to tie you in to that. It is not hard for me to understand the Virgin of Guadalupe, even though I'm a Protestant, because I'm a Chicano.

CHAPTER 5

The Secular-Religious Symbol of
La Raza Cósmica

HISTORICAL PHENOMENA LEADING TO
VASCONCELOS'S CONCEPT OF *LA RAZA CÓSMICA*

Georg Friedrich Nicolai

Georg Friedrich Nicolai, who had a great influence on Vasconcelos, was born in Berlin in 1872. Before the outbreak of World War I, he held the chair of physiology at Berlin University and was known throughout Germany as a leading heart specialist. One of Nicolai's beliefs was that the twilight of the War Gods had come.[1] He also asserted that war is never to be regarded as a necessary and inevitable part of nature wholly beyond human control, something to which we must submit.[2] Nicolai loved Germany as only a true patriot and statesman could. He wrote and spoke against German militarism, patriotism, nationalism, and chauvinism. He openly protested the German Manifesto of October 1914, which was signed by ninety-three representatives of German art and science. For his action he was removed from his professorship and his property was confiscated. He, his wife, and his daughter were left penniless. He was imprisoned in the Graudenz fortress until his escape, arranged by friends, in 1918.

In *The Biology of War* Nicolai, speaking about cosmopolitan patriotism in America, observed its limitations:

> The time for a universal brotherhood has not yet arrived. The clefts which separate the white race from the yellow and black are still too deep. . . . When Americans say, "America for Americans," what they really mean is America for the free descendants of white Europeans. Despite all the enthusiasm for the emancipation of slaves, racial antagonism toward non-Europeans is more marked in America than anywhere else. In the Southern states it often assumes ridiculous and grotesque forms.[3]

This quote is important because José Vasconcelos also saw what Nicolai had observed. Vasconcelos had lived in the United States and had gone to school in Eagle Pass, Texas. His experience of discrimination at the hands of white Texans was never forgotten. Vasconcelos wrote:

> A very significant case which marks a period in the history of our thought I find in the books of Professor Nicolai, who has brought us new biological and racial concepts and perhaps has let himself be absorbed by the Ibero-American milieu, judging from his recent works which have been translated into Spanish. His theories, solidly scientific and contrary to the thesis of the extermination of the weak by the strong and competitive, will someday be the base for all Ibero-American sociology. Confronting Darwinism, which like a destructive poison was given to us by the philosophies of the imperialistic nations, the doctrines of cooperation and mutual help proposed by Nicolai within our midst respond exactly to the social condition of Latin America and to the historical mission which is entrusted to us.[4]

Another important statement by Nicolai:

> If any nation of the present day desires to do something essentially important for the future, it must teach the world to see its own many-colored diversity and it must put it to good account.[5]

Vasconcelos wrote *La Raza Cósmica* (1925) and *Indología* (1927) as a response to Nicolai's suggestion. Nicolai, like any true patriot and statesman, wanted his country, Germany, to be the nation to carry out his vision. Vasconcelos saw the many-colored diversity in Mexico and Latin American. There the indigenous, the African, the Asian, and the European created a *mestizaje* (a mixture of races), the Latin American. Materially, aesthetically, and intellectually, Latin America already had the characteristics of Nicolai's vision: the concept of *La Raza*.[6] Consciousness of *La Raza* and what it entailed would be an essential contribution for the future.

Vasconcelos and Social Darwinism

In the prologue to his revision of *La Raza Cósmica* Vasconcelos stated:

> My book was published for the first time in the period when the Darwinian theory of natural selection which saves the successful and condemns the less successful prevailed in the scientific community; this theory, when taken to the social field by Gobineau, gave rise to the theory of the pure Aryan, defended by the English and taken to an aberrant, deceptive extreme by Nazism.[7]

Also during this period there prevailed in the United States a "cosmic tendency"[8] with its stress on the manifest destiny of the Anglo-Saxons and on the theory of survival of the fittest. Richard Hofstadter states:

> Although Darwinism was not the primary source of the belligerent ideology and dogmatic racism of the late nineteenth century, it did become a new instrument in the hands of the theorists of race and struggle. . . . The Darwinian mood sustained the belief in Anglo-Saxon racial superiority which obsessed many American thinkers in the latter half of the nineteenth century. The measure of world domination already achieved by the "race" seemed to prove it to be the fittest.[9]

Hofstadter quotes two American thinkers who exemplified the extent to which both of these theories were believed. John Fiske of Harvard was one of these men. Hofstadter says:

> With characteristic Darwinian emphasis upon racial fertility, Fiske dwelt upon the great population potential of the English and American races. America could support at least 700,000,000 and the English people would within a few centuries cover Africa with teeming cities, flourishing farms, railroads, telegraphs, and all the devices of civilization. This was the Manifest Destiny of the race. Every land on the globe that was not already the seat of an old civilization should become English in language, traditions, and blood. Four-fifths of the human race would trace its pedigree to English forefathers.[10]

Rev. Josiah Strong was the other American Hofstadter quoted:

> Then will the world enter upon a new stage of its history—*the final competition of races for which the Anglo-Saxon is being schooled*. If I don't read amiss, the powerful race will move down upon Mexico, down upon Central and South America, out upon the islands of the sea, over upon Africa, and beyond. And can anyone doubt that the result of this competition of races will be the survival of the fittest.[11]

Strong's book *Our Country: Its Possible Future and Its Present Crisis* sold 175,000 copies in 1885.[12] The racists of this period adhered to a policy of racial purity, believing that all mixtures of races were inferior.

This "cosmic tendency" of the Anglo-Saxon together with Vasconcelos's earlier experience of racial discrimination created the necessary impulse for him to write *La Raza Cósmica*. The racist attitude of Americans toward Mexicans, even before Darwin's theory, was brought out by Hofstadter in these words:

> At the time when Darwin was still hesitantly outlining his theory in private, racial destiny had already been called upon

by American expansionists to support the conquest of Mexico. The Mexican race now sees in the fate of the aborigines of the North, their own inevitable destiny, an expansionist had written. They must amalgamate or be lost in the superior vigor of the Anglo-Saxon race, or they must utterly perish.[13]

With this attitude carrying over into the twentieth century, it was logical for a Mexican intellectual to rise up and to build up the pride of Latin America's mixture of races. This was the intention of José Vasconcelos with his ideology of *La Raza Cósmica*.

Racism

Racism is a social disease. We have not found a cure for it yet. With *La Raza Cósmica* Vasconcelos initiated an ideology that attempted to find a cure. I believe he was ahead of his time with this ideology in spite of its limitations. It stressed the inclusivity of the four races.

Racism is also a living nightmare. Unlike a nightmare, though, it does destroy. It destroys its victims and it destroys the racists. The best way to end a nightmare is to jump right into it and be devoured if necessary. I have never been devoured by it, but in the process of fighting it, I wake up.

In this living nightmare of racism, we are awake and we can see the victims. We need to jump into this living nightmare and make the necessary preparations to conquer it. It will destroy us unless we destroy it first. We need all the institutions at our disposal to fight racism. The church, the academy, the state, associations, the university, labor, management, conservative and progressive activist groups need to jump into this living nightmare and bring it under control. When we see no equal representation of Blacks, Chicanos, Asians, and native Americans among the personnel in our churches, in our legal systems, in our government, in our academies of art, science, medicine, and music, in all of our decision-making institutions, we are visibly told that racism lives. We need models that stop the exclusion of our fellow men and women whose skin is a different color from ours. We cannot use exclusivistic models to legitimate our racist attitudes toward others. To find new inclusivistic models we need to recall Nicolai's words:

Gladly and gratefully all great Germans have tried to digest and elaborate within themselves the totality of the civilization of their period. Even if no nation is thinkable without foreign influences, this is especially true of Germany. Its civilization is so deep and glorious and original just because it is not autochthonous, but embraces all the world.[14]

The social genius of *La Raza* as Vasconcelos envisioned it was in the model (the attitude) that it embraces the four major races of the world. Whereas Germany's genius was in its inclusivistic music (Bach, Mozart), philosophy (Kant), and literature (Goethe), Latin America's genius is in the social phenomenon of *La Raza*. Vasconcelos recognized the genius of this social phenomenon, which was unique to Latin America. *La Raza*'s contribution was its concept of *mestizaje*. It was an inclusivistic model of social-racial integration.

JOSÉ CALDERÓN VASCONCELOS

José Vasconcelos was a Mexican writer, editor, publisher, statesman, lawyer, educator, intellectual, patriot, and the author of *La Raza Cósmica*. Of all the books he wrote, he is remembered best for this controversial book, a book which up to now has not been translated into English. Vasconcelos is important to the whole question of Chicano identity "because this man has provoked much needed discussion and reflection on who we are" (José Ángel Gutiérrez).

After the Mexican Revolution Vasconcelos was appointed Minister of Education. He extended public education to all Mexicans. His efforts are still felt today by Chicanos who encounter recent Mexican immigrants and see that in spite of fewer years in school the immigrants are often educationally better prepared than many Chicanos in the Southwest. Vasconcelos's endeavors were not in vain.

Vasconcelos ran for president of Mexico but lost, primarily because of his antagonism to and distrust of North Americans, who supported the other Mexican candidate. After the elections Vasconcelos felt that another revolution was necessary, but it never came. Vasconcelos exiled himself to France and traveled extensively in Europe. While residing in Paris he wrote *La Raza Cósmica* (1925) and *Indología* (1927). Both of these books deal with the theme of *La Raza Cósmica*. For his efforts, Vasconcelos has been both praised and criticized.

The ideology of *La Raza Cósmica*, the assertion that the mixture of races does not create inferiority, was a living reality among Hispanic peoples in the New World. Vasconcelos himself was a *mestizo* coming to the aid of other *mestizos*. His thought was similar to the "Black is beautiful" movement in the United States during the late sixties. In trying to prove his point, Vasconcelos ran into trouble when he used the racist model of the eugenicists, with whom he was in dialogue. This model places the white first and the black last in its structure. By coming to our understanding of *La Raza* from the following analysis of our own perspective and within our own dialogue, we will, I hope, build a truer concept of our experience (with its nonracist model) than Vasconcelos, who was dialoguing with racist purists.

DEVELOPING THE THEME OF *LA RAZA CÓSMICA* BY AN ANALYSIS OF THE ORAL TRADITION

The shared theme was presented to the Chicano leaders in this way:

> *José Vasconcelos, a Mexican upper-class intellectual, intro-duced his book* La Raza Cósmica: Misión de la Raza Ibe-roamericana *in 1925. It was first published in Paris. In dealing with race, class, and national issues this book is very controversial. It has not been translated into English.* No le conviene al *Anglo-Saxon* que este libro sea traducido *(it is not to the Anglo-Saxon's advantage that the book be translated into English)—at least not this one from a Mexican neighbor.*
>
> *The imperialistic tendencies of white North Americans are disclosed early in this essay. Vasconcelos wished to find a common ground and a common identity to establish a politi-cal and spiritual cohesion in Latin America, which was being economically ransacked by European and white North American interests.*
>
> *Chicanos, who have been downtrodden for nearly one*

hundred and fifty years in the Southwest, adopted the term
La Raza *as a rallying cry for unity and justice during the late
sixties and early seventies. Chicanos were proud of being
members of* La Raza *once again.*

*In your opinion what are the positive and negative aspects
of this symbolic concept? In our present-day reality of oppression what new light—if any—could we shed on it? Ob-
serving the historical development of this concept, is it a
viable symbol for liberation?*

La Raza as a Symbol of Cosmicity

If intellectuals concern themselves with the mind and intellect of
a people, poets concern themselves with the heart and soul of a
people. Ricardo Sánchez, a Chicano poet, defined cosmicity: "Our
cosmicity comes from within us." According to Sánchez that cosmicity is our humanity, our universality; it is that within us that
makes us who we are. You cannot go outside yourself and find that
reality which is you. That reality must be found within you.

You go into yourself, you delve into yourself for all answers
not because you are an oracle, but because it is all within you
as a person and you find what there is about you and makes
you you. You strengthen it; you nurture it; and you develop it
to express it so that you can share it with others, especially
with those that you love.

Sánchez's concept of cosmicity concerns itself with the essence of
a person. What makes this individual who he or she is? What is
universal to him or her that is universal to all humankind? What
does a Chicano have that is common to everyone else? What makes
a person dream, wish? What makes a human being, and why is a
person a human being? Cosmicity is a way to express this essence. It
is a concept that makes one inclusive with the universe. It is a
symbol that ties us together to our own essence and helps us to
fulfill and live our own reality without fear or intimidation.

But a lot of Chicanos believe it is not within themselves, but
out there. Vasconcelos was caught in that trap. A lot of

Mexican intellectuals were looking outward. They looked to Europe, they looked everywhere but within themselves. That's a fault of Vasconcelos in the sense that in the process of identifying himself, he leaned too far toward Europe to find the answer.

Sánchez teaches us a valuable lesson in these two quotations. You do not go to someone else for confirmation of your own reality. No one can do that for you. How can someone in Europe (if you are white North American), in Africa (if you are a Black North American) confirm your reality? Only you living this experience in North America know that reality.

Some of the oppressed who are treated as nonbeings believe that in order to be, they have to prove themselves to the "beings" in the status quo. The tragedy of this enterprise is that in the process of trying to confirm yourself you lose your own reality; you adapt to the models of the status quo and consequently you forfeit your own identity. Your identity can only be given by the models engendered by your own experience. As a consequence you do not liberate yourself; instead you assimilate into something else. Frantz Fanon's book *Black Skin, White Masks* is a classic critique of Blacks who forfeit their own Black reality by trying to be white.

So I see Sánchez giving the concept of *La Raza Cósmica* a greater dimension. Instead of going outward to Europe, to Spain, to the abstract, to the aesthetics, he goes inward to the *indio*, to the Mexican, to the North American, to the innermost spiritual depths of our identity as Chicanos. Only a poet can express that. Sánchez also tells us: "Whatever theology we as Chicanos are going to have someday is going to be created from within ourselves."

I believe when the Roman Catholic missionary brings Roman Catholicism to colonized natives, it is the duty of colonized natives to change Roman Catholicism to native Catholicism. Only by this spiritual act can they decolonize and speed up the process of liberation, which is the process toward salvation. It is difficult for the missionary to bring salvation to the oppressed without the good news of liberation. Moses was a liberator because he led the people out of a situation of oppression. Jesus Christ is a liberator because he came to liberate the oppressed. In Jesus' time one wonders who was responsible for the greatest oppression—the Roman legions or the Jewish hierarchy. In Latin and North America, one wonders who is responsible for the greatest oppression—the military democracies or the church hierarchy, which does not denounce the military budget.

Cosmicity is a symbol not only of self-revelation (revealing oneself) but also of self-criticism. How and why did we get into this oppressive situation and when do we get out? This question, like the symbol of cosmicity, formulates the foundation of a process toward liberation.

La Raza Cósmica as a Symbol of *Auto-Identificarse* (Identifying Oneself)

> *Es importante para nosotros usar la palabra "raza" hoy en día porque uno tiene que primeramente auto-identificarse. Uno para poder ser tiene que saber quien es y para saber quien es, es muy sencillo: uno se dice quien es; uno se da su propia identidad.*

It is important for us to use the word *raza* nowadays because we have to first identify ourselves. In order to be we have to know who we are and in order to know who we are—it is very simple—we tell ourselves who we are, give ourselves our own identity.

José Ángel Gutiérrez introduces here an important biblical attribute of human beings. In Genesis 2:19–20 we find Yahweh bringing the cattle, the birds of the heavens, and all the wild beasts to the first human being to name them. Hence one of the first human responsibilities was to designate everything by naming it. Difficult as it may seem, man/woman also have the responsibility of naming themselves.

> *Soy cobarde; soy buen amigo; soy trabajador; uno se da su propia identidad.*

I am a coward; I am a good friend; I am a worker; we give ourselves our own identity.

Therefore Gutiérrez tells us that we tell others who we are by naming ourselves. In the process of knowing who we are we name ourselves. Who are we? As a group we are a mixture of the European and the indigenous. *Somos raza, la raza.*

Gutiérrez tells us that it took Mexico almost four hundred years to overthrow the political yoke of Spain only to incur the economic-political yoke of France and the United States.

> *No ha tenido México todavía su propia tranquilidad para desarollarse como país, como pueblo. Y nosotros [los Chicanos] que somos descendentes de esas gentes sufrimos igual.*

> Mexico has not yet had its own tranquility to develop itself as a nation, as a people. And we [Chicanos] who are descendants of those people suffer equally.

Chicanos have inherited the sufferings that Mexico experienced.

Gutiérrez admits that we are not yet the cosmic race because as an oppressed group of people it is difficult to reach out of oppression and to show the dynamic and the potential of which we are capable. Nevertheless by *auto-identificándonos* we have taken the first step towards liberation—a step that is not only social and political but also theological. It addresses the theological problem of naming who we are. *Somos mestizos. Somos la raza.*

La Raza Cósmica as a Symbol of Mestizaje

The Chicano community by its presence, in spite of the colonial conquest in North America, is a viable political and human force. Its focus in history is on the manipulation of the rich countries and the exploitation of the oppressed.

> We are a mixture of the two, the Hispanic and the gringo. This is the Chicano experience today [Msgr. Longinus Reyes].

> Vasconcelos was trying to put across that Hispanics represent all the rainbow of colors of people, that once you are brought into the family, once you belong to the family of *La Raza*,

color is not an issue. There is something more than color that binds you [Rubén Armendariz].

The blending of two races, two cultures, is really demonstrated by a strong social and political situation. That to me is of spiritual significance [Lupe Anguiano].

GUERRERO: So the *La Raza* concept is real to us in the sense that it's a symbol of unity, right?

TIJERINA: Of course, Andrés, yes, *La Raza*, but you have to be careful because by *La Raza* you can also mean the new breed of the Spanish and the Indian, but I do not think so. I don't think that's *La Raza*. I think *La Raza* is the one that absorbed the other one. When the Spaniards came here, they gave their name to the Indian. The Indian did not absorb the Spaniard. Now, *La Raza*, the children of Joseph, left Palestine and went to Spain. There they did the same thing they did here. They absorbed the tribes of Spain. They imposed their thought, mentality, spirituality, their doctrine, and their religion on their tribes. They did this because the Hebrews, the Israelite religion, believed faith and monumental history were stronger and more acceptable than what the tribes had in the Iberian Peninsula. So when *La Raza* came here, they repeated it. They give. They absorb. Intermarrying with the Indian only shows that *La Raza* was flexible and had a mission and was not racist. We have Law II, Title I, Book VI of The Laws of the Indies given, I think, on October 19, 1514. In that year, 1514, that law was issued to *La Raza* to legalize marriage between Spanish and Indian.

Anguiano, Reyes, and Armendariz all agree that the mixture is a positive one. I understand that both the Spanish side and Indian side carry equal weight in creating the *mestizo*. Reyes carries this one dimension further. He sees the contribution of the Chicano as a *mestizo* with *el corazón de la raza*; this combines with the impulse of the gringo.[15] In other words the *latinoamericano mestizo* is different from the Chicano *mestizo* in that the Chicano lives in a gringo society.

Sometimes in talking with people from Latin America, when they first become aware of this *raza* within the United States, they get excited about it. They had not thought who Chicanos were really. Yet these Chicanos live with these people, and are getting their thought, their education, their attitudes and all that. But nonetheless, *el corazón es nuestro.* To think not only for *La Raza* but for all people because I think that is just the way we are. We are not going to accumulate everything for ourselves but also for others. Because we just don't hoard things. We share with others, and I might be simplifying the whole thing of *La Raza*, but it is there. I think this is really the redemption, the salvation, of the human race [Msgr. Longinus Reyes].

He [Vasconcelos] is suggesting that this *Raza Cósmica* is really that next step in the evolutionary process. We are really at the apex of industrialization whether it is capitalism or communism or regardless of what it is; there is still the disregard for the sacred, for the sanctity of nature, which of course means the disregard for human life because that is part of nature. We have gotten to that point and by recognizing that there is a *Raza Cósmica*, we have something to contribute and it is not just liberation from oppression [Tomás Atencio].

The contribution that Chicanos have to offer has to do with human relationships. *Mestizaje* is a synthesis, a combination, an inclusivity of human interrelationships. With industrialization the dehumanizing process has been accelerated. But *mestizaje* replaces the sacredness, the sanctity, the regard for human life. Life, human relationships, are at the foundation of *La Raza Cósmica*. *Mestizaje* is the bridge between black and white (Dolores Huerta).

The success we have had in blending two races, two cultures, could be a positive factor in the social and economic development of the world community (Lupe Anguiano). *Mestizaje* works. It accomplishes through action what humanists believe in theory. Two different races can marry and make it work provided they see the process of liberation going on. Two cultures can blend to create a new humanity different from the two parents.

The *mestizaje* of a communist and a capitalist would bring about a new person. The *mestizaje* of the oppressor and the oppressed would bring about a new person, neither oppressor nor oppressed but a blending of the two. The good from both would predominate. If the evil from both predominated, it would be a disaster.[16] Thinking positively, if the good predominated it would give rise to a new political being whose interests in all of this would be the concern for human life.

La Raza as a Symbol of Hope

> The Chicanos could be the hope for the whole hemisphere. First *el corazón* is *hispano*, *el corazón* is *latino*, *el corazón* is of *La Raza*. Second, because of our experience here our influence is gringo [Msgr. Longinus Reyes].

Chicanos can be a hope because they relate to both the *latino* world and the gringo world. They can be a bridge bringing these two cultures together. They can relate to the affluent world because they live in it and they can relate to the impoverished world because they are poor. For Chicanos *corazón* is the concern for humanity, for life, for loved ones, and for *compadres* and *comadres* (godparents of your children).

It is not uncommon to hear Chicanos use the cordial and amicable word *pobrecito* in regard to Somoza or Nixon. They feel sorry for these individuals because they (Somoza or Nixon) have lost contact with reality. Reality is life and the other person. Once you forget reality you live in a vacuum with no *amistades* (friends). *Amistades* and having *corazón* are essential to the Chicano, Latino, Hispanic culture. To stay in touch with reality you have to stay in touch with your *amistades*, your family, even your enemies. You have to acknowledge and respect everyone.

José Ángel Gutíerrez described well the church, coopted by the growers and exploiters, but you can see *corazón* in his response: "Can you imagine if the personnel and the business of the church sided with the oppressed? My God, it would be the most powerful, beautiful movement in history."

Chicanos never lose hope that evil will eventually be overtaken by the good. This hope is not only Christian European but also indigenous. Native Americans have a strong sense of harmony, honesty, and justice. When their egos and selfish imperialistic tendencies took possession of them they oppressed other tribes.

Together with this *corazón*, warmth for others, is the gringo impulse. Chicanos have been educated in Anglo-Saxon schools; we learned their administrative skills and technology; we know the gringo thought, their stereotypes, their attitudes. We live with the gringo. We have adopted many of their strengths and sad to say even their weaknesses. But our *corazón latino* gives our gringo impulse a deeper meaning because of our warmth for humanity, for the *compadrazgo*.

La Raza as a Symbol of Unity

Tomás Atencio said this:

> *La Raza* is a unifying factor in terms of masses and mass movements of Hispanos, where it manifests itself first as a very real phenomenon. People feel it. That is at the structural level. . . . Most would rather say *raza* than Chicano. This is basically accepted. It is the unifying principle of the people who are not doing too much reflection. But it is also a unifying principle intellectually.

Tomás Atencio tells us that for Hispanos, the key word for unity is *La Raza*. All the Hispanos—Cubans, Puerto Ricans, Chicanos, Mexicans, Central Americans, South Americans, Spanish-speaking Caribbeans—are all *La Raza*. Not only Hispanos can unite under this symbolic concept; all of Latin America can unite under this concept. It is a powerful concept because of the unifying strength it carries.

One does not have to be an intellectual to understand its political implication. *La Raza* includes the cosmicity of all the blood mixtures possible. The mixtures were acknowledged by the Spaniards, who coined words such as *mestizos* and *mulatos* for the purpose of legitimizing them in a racist society.

The spiritual-secular symbol of *La Raza* is not a racist phenomenon per se. Whether Chicanos are *trigueño* (very dark) or *güero* (blond), they are still Chicano. They are still members of *La Raza*. Cubans and Puerto Ricans, while still on the islands, are Cubans and Puerto Ricans, but as soon as they land in the United States they are either black Cuban or black Puerto Rican or white Cuban or white Puerto Rican. I have never heard the terms black *raza* or white *raza*. Those terms would destroy the whole concept of *La Raza*. They would destroy the secular-spiritual unity that *La Raza* nurtures.

In English the word "race" implies color, but in *La Raza* color is not stressed. The beauty of *La Raza Cósmica* lies in its literal color-blindness. The Anglo-Saxon has a tendency to judge your humanity by the color of your skin and by the position that you hold. But in *La Raza* you are judged by the size of your *corazón*, by how well you do a job and how much pride you take in doing it, regardless of how menial or how long it takes you to accomplish it. For *La Raza* time is not money; it is sacred.

La Raza as a Symbol of New Creation

Rubén Armendariz has this to tell us about *La Raza*.

Theologically, for me, it has a certain eschatological dimension. One thinks about the Kingdom of God as a reality when people will not see those differences. I think about it in terms of the New Creation. What does Paul say about a New Creation? We are all the family of God. Does the family of God speak in terms of racial groups, in terms of ethnic groups, in terms of color? No, it speaks about a whole family of God in a diversity. In a contemporary sense, if we want to speak about a New Creation, Vasconcelos had it in a very secular way, *La Raza Cósmica*. For me that is very powerful. I like to put it in contemporary terms. In a paper I wrote I alluded to the fact that this presents a whole new dimension, particularly for those who want to talk about white supremacy. One cannot talk that way in New Testament terms, not even in Old Testament terms.

So it is important for me to press the idea that Vasconcelos had. I'm reminded of Paul in Galatians: in Christ there are no Jews, no Greeks, no Romans, no men, no women, but we're all one in Christ. In a way that is a New Creation. Hispanos (*La Raza*) represent that New Creation in society because they cut across lines.

GUERRERO: Vasconcelos established a hierarchy of values with the whites first and the blacks at the end. In his concept of *La Raza* he unintentionally falls into the trap by presupposing that white is superior to black. Would you address that issue?

ARMENDARIZ: One cannot get into his life, or understand why he did that. The theme of *La Raza Cósmica* in itself is not racist.

GUERRERO: Is it a natural phenomenon or a natural conclusion?

ARMENDARIZ: It is a natural conclusion if we were to follow all our natural instincts. In other words, if we were not to look at either class, status, or racial groups in relationship to other people, it would follow as a natural conclusion. Though I recognize that Vasconcelos had a hierarchial understanding where, at least in his own thinking, he was striving to articulate what an ideal would be, what a utopia would be that would include everyone—in the back of his mind, as I try to understand him he sees a mixing that is inevitable. That is what people who subscribe to a particular superiority of one race would not like to hear. Vasconcelos has a lot to say in *La Raza Cósmica* that will bring us all together. Hispanos have that, so I think he had a great ideal to offer. I would like to tie it with the theme of the New Creation and the Kingdom of God, which I don't think has been done yet.

Armendariz presents an enlightened theological proposition to us. What would be the theological outcome of a mixing of the races? Westerners have always been tempted to preserve racial purity and white values. If we adhere to our racial prejudices, how do we know that we are not postponing the coming of the Kingdom?

La Raza as a Symbol of Liberation

Msgr. Longinus Reyes tells us:

How to really penetrate the enemy's mind, to learn who they are and how they are, to be part of that and get to work within that, instead of running around the fort like our ancestors did. We are already inside, and we know what the strategy is, what the whole attitude is, what the whole plan is. To me this is the exciting part of this whole concept of *La Raza*. But yet, as a Chicano, knowing the system, the technology, knowing whatever needs to be known because I'm part of it, I live it, I am able to work toward a more equitable and a more just society because to me that is what *La Raza* is. In that sense I would see it as something that would bring about a liberation.

Msgr. Reyes is telling us that Chicanos as members of *La Raza* have tremendous input into the process of liberation. This *raza* concept of liberation is very close to the communion of saints and the Body of Christ teachings, which advocate a just society. In that sense the symbol of *La Raza* has a great contribution to make toward the redemption and the salvation of the human race. This is a further development of the *corazón* concept Reyes believes Chicanos as *La Raza* possess.

Lupe Anguiano tells us:

There is no doubt in my mind that we present a challenge to the gringo's treatment of the Native American. They came and they tried to destroy Native Americans whereas the colonization of Spain into Mexico brought the development of a new race. I believe that the world is the better for it. *La Raza* is a demonstration of a strong social and political situation because of the blending of two races, two cultures. To me that is of spiritual significance. That experience, that phenomenon has not been treated adequately by our educational, cultural, and intellectual centers.

The phenomenon of *La Raza*, of the mixture of peoples, needs to be developed to encourage inclusivity and equality among peoples. To believe that one race is better than another race is to misinterpret the New Testament. It is also a presumptuous attitude that no one ought to tolerate. One reason the Mexican (*mestizo*) could not get along with the Spaniard (*gachupín*) was the arrogance of the Spaniard. Chicanos cannot get along with gringos because of the arrogance of the gringo. In relationship to Chicanos, *gachupínes* and gringos have a lot in common. Once gringos or *gachupínes* think they are better than another race they can legitimize anything, even genocide.

Historically wars of conquest, the Spanish Inquisition, the Jewish Holocaust were probably caused by some form of secular or religious superiority complex. The concept of *La Raza Cósmica* tries to tone this arrogance down so that we can control it instead of it controlling us.

José Ángel Gutiérrez tells us:

I believe we are a people who have suffered much, who have been oppressed much, who need much in order to develop as a vibrant people. For centuries ours has been a struggle for liberation. From the indigenous side, to create our situation of oppression came the most opportunistic and the most imperialistic of the colonizers to put us down. We fought almost four centuries against the Spaniards so as to remove their *gachupín* influences. Then it took almost another hundred years for Mexico to find its identity and place in the sun and the Mexican revolution started. At this time the gringos and the French came in with their influences. Mexico is still struggling trying to get rid of these foreign influences. Mexico has not yet had the proper tranquility to develop itself as a nation.

Being descendants of the Mexicans, we Chicanos suffer the same way they do. *Nosotros somos la piel donde toca el cuerpo mexicano al pueblo norteamericano y a los demás pueblos. Y nosotros sufrimos más como le pasa a la piel—se quema, se enfría, bueno, le pasa toda clase de cosas.*[17] It is there where all the disasters happen. I do not believe that we are part of a *raza cósmica* yet because we have not even had a chance to move forward like a people in order to show the dynamic or the potential that we are capable of.

José Ángel Gutiérrez tells us that those foreign influences, those oppressive role models have to be reckoned with and brought under control. People, nations, need a chance to develop. Chicanos, Mexicans cannot possibly show the world the dynamic or the potential that they are capable of if their history is one of concern for survival. Who has time to develop if they are always defending their right to exist? Existence for the oppressed is a battle to survive. Once survival is insured, then we can begin to contribute. Liberation means that you fight to survive and that you insure your place in the sun by contributing to the world community.

We are in a position to contribute a great deal to the world because we are the *piel* (skin) of the problem between the impoverished nations and the affluent nations. We are one entity, but a people living two realities. We have one foot in the rich world and one in the poor world. We experience both because we live both. Racially we are all the different colors of people. Economically we are poor in a rich country. Politically we are millions of people but invisible. Culturally we are a combination of four major cultures. Socially we interact with many people who have also been mixed and look like us. Spiritually, because of our *mestizaje*, we have characteristics that encounter and include others.

CONCLUSION

Although Vasconcelos rejected the claims of the racial purists by showing that *La Raza* was not inferior, he took part in their dialogue and used their eugenic models to develop his ideology.

Chicanos who dialogue among themselves in their experience of oppression use models from their own perspective of reality to develop the concept of *La Raza Cósmica*. Instead of turning to Europe for models they delve into themselves for new nonracist models. *La Raza* as a symbol of cosmicity is an inclusivistic model that ties us to our own essence and helps us to fulfill and live our own reality. *La Raza* as a symbol of *auto-identificarse* addresses the theological problem of naming who we are: *somos mestizos, somos La Raza.*

As a symbol of *mestizaje*, *La Raza* for Chicanos is an inclusivity of human interrelationships. Included in this *mestizaje* is the *corazón latino* and the gringo impulse. As a symbol of hope, *La Raza* helps us to fight against despair. As a symbol of unity, it is a unifying principle for all Chicanos and all Latin Americans. As a symbol of the New Creation, it stresses that amid all our diversity we are one in Christ. As a symbol of liberation, *La Raza* struggles to survive as the *piel* between the impoverished nations and the affluent nations.

CHAPTER 6

Conclusions and Perspectives

Having analyzed Guadalupe (chapter 4) and *La Raza Cósmica* (chapter 5), I must now show how these two symbols can help in the development of a Chicano theology of liberation. In his book *Farewell to Innocence* Allan Boesak tells us that the central theme of liberation is to be found in Luke 4:18–19.[1] In this passage Jesus said:

> The Spirit of the Lord has been given to me,
> for he has anointed me.
> He has sent me to bring the good news to the poor,
> to proclaim liberty to captives
> and to the blind new sight,
> to set the downtrodden free,
> to proclaim the Lord's year of favor [JB].

This is the same message of liberation that I set out to address in the symbols Guadalupe and *La Raza Cósmica*. In spite of the good news of liberation proclaimed in Luke, Chicanos continue to be exploited. By comparing the message of Luke with the message of Guadalupe and the concept of *La Raza Cósmica*, both Guadalupe and *La Raza Cósmica* can be redefined and translated as symbols of liberation in the development of a Chicano theology. Redefining our symbols will change our experience from one of oppression toward one that recognizes a process of liberation.

138

First I will set out the essential elements of a Chicano theology as derived from an analysis of the experience of the leaders I interviewed.

A COMPARATIVE ANALYSIS OF LUKE 4:18–19 AND THE PROMISES OF *NUESTRA SEÑORA DE GUADALUPE*

The *Nican Mopohua* is the earliest known text on the apparition of *Nuestra Señora de Guadalupe* and her promises to Juan Diego. The Nahuatl text is attributed to Don Antonio Valeriano, a teacher at Colegio de Santa Cruz de Tlatelolco.[2] The text is in the Nahuatl language of the Aztecs. The translation of the text from the Nahuatl to the Spanish is by Dr. Don Ángel M. Garibay K. I have translated pertinent passages into English.

By comparing Luke 4:18–19 and the *Nican Mopohua* (see chart below) I propose to show how the message of liberation relates to both. Luke stresses liberation from oppression. The *Nican Mopohua* also emphasizes the theme of liberation, even though historically only the aspect of alleviation from physical necessity has been stressed by the church. The apparition gave the native American the political reason to survive and to rebel against complete domination by the Spanish. Under the symbol of Guadalupe this political encounter was reenacted in the war for independence and in the Mexican Revolution.

Luke 4:18–19 and the Guadalupe Text (*Nican Mopohua*)

Luke 4:18–19	*Nican Mopohua*	*Nican Mopohua*
The spirit of the Lord has been given to me, for he has anointed me.	23. I am the perfect and perpetual Virgin Mary, Mother of the true God.	25. I am your compassionate mother, of you and all of you who live united in this land, and of all the various different peoples who love me, who cry mournfully

		to me, who look for me, who hold me in their confidence.
He has sent me to bring the good news to the poor,	24. I want very much and with intimate desire that on this place a temple be built in my honor.	26. There I will hear their cries, their afflictions,
to proclaim liberty to captives and to the blind new sight, to set the downtrodden free, to proclaim the Lord's year of favor.	There I will show, I will manifest, I will give all my love, I will give all my love, my compassion, my help, my defense for humankind.	so as to liberate, to heal their multiple anguishes, needs, and miseries. 28. Tell [the Bishop] heartily all that you have seen, witnessed, and that which you have heard.

In Luke 4:18–19 we have Jesus receiving the Spirit of the Lord. Verse 23 of the *Nican Mopohua* identifies the perfect and perpetual Virgin Mary, Mother of the true God; verse 25 reidentifies her as a compassionate mother of all those who are in need and affliction and who have confidence in her.

In Luke we read: "He has sent me to bring the good news to the poor." Verse 24 of the *Nican Mopohua* states "that on this place a temple be built in my honor." Verse 26 says that this is where persons can come to ask the Virgin for assistance. In Luke we find the proclamation of liberty to captives, of sight to the blind, and of the Lord's year of favor. The downtrodden will be set free. In the *Nican Mopohua* we see that Guadalupe will give love, compassion, help, and defense to humankind. In verse 26 she promises "to hear their cries, their affliction, so as to liberate, to heal their multiple anguishes, needs, and miseries."

All of these are signs of hope to the oppressed. There is a clear analogy between Jesus' mission as the son of God in regard to the poor and Guadalupe's mission in regard to the poor. Both convey messages of spiritual and physical liberation. Both were sent by God to alleviate the fate of the downtrodden. Both came to help those with the greatest need.

Judging from the Lukan passage we can say that Jesus is the liberator of the oppressed; judging from the *Nican Mopohua* we can say that Guadalupe, as the mother of the oppressed, is also a liberator. Both came for the purpose of performing positive actions in history. However, the Lukan passage is more political than the *Nican Mopohua*. The *Nican Mopohua* stresses the alleviation of present hardships and miseries. The Lukan passage stresses the elimination of the political conditions of misery. In the section on the poor (see below), we will see that the mistreatment of the downtrodden in ancient and biblical times brought political reprimand to those who abused and oppressed them.

There is a theology in the New Testament that can be applied to the Chicano situation. It is found in the Magnificat in Luke's infancy narrative.

GUADALUPE AND THE MAGNIFICAT

The core of the Magnificat contrasts the different fates of the proud/mighty/rich and the lowly/hungry; the former are scattered, put down, and sent away hungry, while the latter are exalted and filled (1:51-53). In all the Synoptic Gospels, Jesus addresses himself to the outcasts; but Luke places a special emphasis on those who are "on the periphery," the downtrodden, sinners, women, widows, Samaritans (7:11-7, 36-50; 10:29-37; 17:11-19).[3]

In particular, it has been suggested that Mary is a representative of the piety of the Anawim, the "Poor Ones." This term may have originally designated the economically poor (and frequently still included them), but it came to refer widely to those who could not trust in their own strength: the downtrodden, the poor, the lowly, the afflicted, the widows and orphans.[4]

The Spaniard, the oppressor, was politically dominant in Latin America. The native American was conquered and consequently oppressed. The intermarriage of the two created a new people. In a sense we can say that this union brought down the mighty and raised up the lowly. This does not mean that native Americans are no longer oppressed. They still are. Nor does it prove that their oppression exists because many native Americans did not intermarry with the Spanish. Why native Americans are still oppressed is an open question. Those who did marry Spaniards created a *mestizaje*.

This *mestizaje*, a union by the intermarriage of Spaniard (oppressor) and native American (oppressed), created a new cosmic experience: the Mexican and the Chicano. For Chicanos this was an experience of oppression because *mestizos* have been treated as native Americans and have not been given the political and economic opportunity to pull out of their oppression. The high and proud have been brought down and the lowly have been raised up by their union. It is hoped that the idea of a new socialism will arise from the Chicano experience, a socialism that can be based in the Magnificat.

Guadalupe, symbolic of Chicano hope, can be an instrument of strengthening the union, of bringing down the high and mighty and raising up the lowly. Nurturing this concept in our experience, we can establish a balance between the oppressor and the oppressed. Theologically, this could give rise to a new socialism operating from the Chicano experience. This is a phenomenon of race (all four races are represented), of class (the rich/mighty are brought down and the lowly/hungry raised up), of color (we are of all different colors), and of sex (the role of women through Guadalupe and through the role of mother is exalted). Through the symbol of Guadalupe Chicanos have experienced a unique transformation that theologically is worth investigating.

Theologically the transformation is unique because two world realities came to fruition within the *mestizo* culture. The mighty (the Spanish) and the lowly (the native Americans) achieved a new social level that addresses the theology of the Magnificat.

Guadalupe, as a Chicano symbol of faith and hope, helps us apply that theology to our own cosmic-universal reality. She ties us in to that theology with her concern for the oppressed. If her concern is for the oppressed, then in some way the mighty must be brought down, just as the Spaniards were. Through the theology of the Magnificat Guadalupe as a symbol of liberation opens for us a new social vision where oppressors and oppressed can merge to create a new humanity, more just and with a greater *corazón*.

THE SOCIOCULTURAL, POLITICAL, ECONOMIC, AND SPIRITUAL IMPACT OF GUADALUPE ON THE LUKAN MESSAGE OF LIBERATION

Guadalupe as a symbol of liberation gives us our identity as social and cultural beings in society. In the liberation process the need to know where one's place is under the sun is important. Guadalupe, the Virgin *Morena*, symbolizes our social and cultural specialness. Mexicans and Chicanos are a special people because Guadalupe selected them to bring forth her message to the oppressed and downtrodden (Dolores Huerta). Socially and culturally, Guadalupe helps to bring the central theme of liberation to fruition by taking on our identity as *mestizos*.

The political significance of the symbol of Guadalupe lies in its unifying strength. Chicanos are all familiar with the image of Guadalupe as the nurturing mother who does not abandon us when we need her. Unity is necessary for organization and for building up a resistance against forces that impede our liberation. No liberation movement can succeed without the unity and cooperation of the group. Both Catholic and Protestant Chicanos can unite and organize themselves using Guadalupe as their symbolic banner. Guadalupe sides with those who are tortured, raped, and murdered by repressive governments. Politically, Guadalupe sides with the oppressed.

Economically Guadalupe is against capitalism. She cannot condone the actions of the growers and multinational corporations. She condemns their actions because of the exploitation and the institutionalized violence they impose upon the wretched of the earth. Because of the inequalities democratic capitalism brings to the different-colored peoples in this hemisphere, she is more apt to choose some type of socialist government as an option for the poor. In terms of the economic margin for Chicanos in the United States, Guadalupe is a symbol of resistance against exploitative and unjust wages. She symbolizes direct action against the unequal distribution of resources and goods. For Chicanos, the symbol of Guadalupe is against the hoarding of material possessions. To share everything we own is imitative of her generosity toward us. She promised that no sigh, no matter how small, would go unheard.

The spiritual implication is that she listens to the cries of the downtrodden and heals them. Faith in her, our spiritual mother, strengthens our faith in Jesus Christ. A symbol of hope, she is our strength against despair. The impact of this symbol is in the forefront of the Chicano struggle toward liberation. As mother of the Suffering Servant, she is also a mother of all suffering servants on earth. Finally, just as Jesus is a miracle worker in the gospels, so is Guadalupe a miracle worker among Mexicans, Chicanos, and those who believe in her as the mediator between humanity and God.

LOS POBRES (THE POOR)

"The subjects of the kingdom are not men in general, or men in the abstract, but rather the lepers, the lame, the sinners, the lowly worker, in other words 'the poor.'"[5] The poor have always been controversial because they have been so misunderstood.

There are two categories of poor people. The lame, the blind, the mentally retarded, the crippled, the lepers, the brain-damaged are one category. These we will always have with us because of natural causes or accidents. These are also those of whom Jesus spoke when he said: "You have the poor with you always" (Mt 26:11). The other category of poor are the victims of institutionalized violence. They are made poor by human greed and acts of self-interest. Among these are generation after generation of impoverished human beings. Blacks, Chicanos, Latin Americans, Africans, Asians, and impoverished whites in the United States and all over the world fall into this category. Exploitation of their natural resources, their person, and their labor creates this category of *los pobres*.

Both categories of *los pobres* are close to the concept of the kingdom of heaven of which Jesus speaks in the beatitudes. "How happy are the poor in spirit; theirs is the kingdom of heaven" (Mt 5:3).

The poor are called blessed in Mt 5:3; Lk 6:20; Mt has "poor in spirit," a much tortured phrase. It does not mean detachment, but reflects the OT words cited above [see citation below], which it makes explicit; the poor in spirit are the lowly classes, whose spirit is crushed by their need and by oppression. . . . The revolutionary character of this statement should not be missed; the curse of poverty is removed by it, and the blessing consists in the kingdom of heaven, which surpasses all wealth.[6]

The code of the covenant, Israel's earliest collection of law, contains statutes which protect the poor. The debtor who sells himself into slavery must be liberated without any compensation after six years (Ex 21:2). In the sabbatical year the fields are to be left fallow, and the poor may eat what grows there (Ex 23:10f.). Judges must not pervert justice due to the poor (Ex 23:6). More fundamentally, Yahweh is declared to be the avenger of all needy classes (Ex 22:21–24).[7]

One more citation concerning the poor must be added that antedates any Old Testament saying about poverty by at least several centuries.

What the poor could legitimately expect was that the wealthy would not take advantage of them, particularly by using their wealth to corrupt the administration of the government and the processes of justice. This ideal appears as far back as the code of Hammurabi, who says that he was appointed king by Enlil "to cause justice to prevail in the land, to destroy the wicked and the evil, that the strong might not oppress the weak" (ANET 164). His laws are promulgated "in order that the strong might not oppress the weak . . . to give justice to the oppressed" (ANET 178). . . . In Egypt also there was a consciousness of the rights of the poor. The instruction of Merikare warns that the king should not show partiality against the poor in selecting candidates for office (ANET 415). The wisdom of Anenemope . . . warns the rich not to be greedy for the property of a poor man (ANET 423) and urges him to forgive 2/3 of the debt of the poor man (ANET *ibid.*).[8]

We have become so sophisticated and blind in our nuclear age toward the subject of *los pobres* that instead of a rich person being greedy for the property of a poor person, now we have whole nations greedy for the property of impoverished nations. Multinationals, nuclear weapons, cosmic tendencies—all these evils created by human greed legitimize the oppression of the weak.

From the citations above we discover that even the ancients respected the rights of the downtrodden. In their pagan religions they could foresee that justice to the oppressed was a necessity. The Israelites had a consciousness that Yahweh would avenge the poor. It should come as no surprise to us that in the New Testament the kingdom of heaven is made up of the poor in spirit, the downtrodden, those whom no one really cares for, those who have nothing to lose because they possess nothing other than their persons.

The modern world with its technology and communication systems ought to allow for more sensitivity to the needs of the poor than did the ancient world of the Mesopotamians, Egyptians, and Israelites. Yet the distance between rich and poor is becoming more and more pronounced. Ecclesiastically and politically, the poor are voiceless. The poor nations are a clear majority in the United Nations, yet the five rich powers control by their veto power the will of the majority. Geopolitically, priorities for these five nations concern their own national security and economic interests rather than any confrontation with issues of poverty and exploitation. That security and those interests are a high price to pay for peace as poverty and exploitation continue and as even God the Avenger of the oppressed seems against us.

GUADALUPE: OPPRESSIVE OR LIBERATING?

Just as symbols can be used to oppress a people, they can also be used to liberate them. By way of conclusion I would like to point out some ambiguities and some potential dangers inherent in using the symbol of Guadalupe.

Guadalupe is the symbol of symbols in the Chicano experience, yet she has been used by unscrupulous state and church officials to placate and pacify Chicanos. In the name of Guadalupe, poor Mexicans and Chicanos have been kept oppressed, in their place, marginated, and on the periphery of human existence.

But Miguel Hidalgo y Costilla, Emiliano Zapata, and César Chávez have used the symbol of Guadalupe to move the people because they recognized the process of liberation going on and the powerful influence Guadalupe could have in such a process. Guadalupe for them was a powerful symbol to be used to move the oppressed against their oppressors.

Similarly, a Chicano theology can emphasize the power of Guadalupe as a liberating influence provided that the people realize that the process of liberation is going on. If the people do not realize that the process is happening, then the symbol will continue to be used against them. If this is the case, then a Chicano theology urges that the Chicano leaders who recognize the process of liberation translate that message to their people. A Chicano theology insists that church leaders who read the signs of the times ought not to betray their people by keeping the liberating significance of Guadalupe from them. Guadalupe historically has been, can, and ought to be used as part of the *grito* (cry, shout) to unify Chicanos in their struggle toward liberation. Chicano leaders, as servants of their oppressed community, can use the symbol of Guadalupe to denounce the injustices, to reannounce the good news, and to help in re-creating a new society for their victimized community. A Chicano theology supports that endeavor as a necessary one.

Concerning *machismo*, a word of caution must be given in using Guadalupe as a symbol. Historically, Guadalupe has signified our Virgin (redeemed) Mother as opposed to our violated (Indian) mother. Chicano males have hidden behind the Virgin Mother (Guadalupe). They, through their actions, have permitted *machismo* to exist as a tool of oppression against Chicanas. If males do not recognize the process of liberation going on in regard to women, then it is the duty of Chicanas and responsible Chicano leaders to announce the process of liberation, which defends the equality and dignity of women.

A Chicano theology supports this announcement. It also maintains that the symbol of Guadalupe cannot be used in opposition to the violated mother. Males cannot "hail" Mary and then turn around and oppress women. Chicano theology could not condone this contradiction. In Chicano theology, Guadalupe, as a symbol of liberation, is the Mother of all the oppressed. Women as specific victims in every culture hold a special place and have an important

148 *Oral Tradition*

mission to announce their liberation. Guadalupe can be used as a powerful symbol of liberation by women. It is in this direction that a Chicano theology ought to develop.

A COMPARATIVE ANALYSIS OF LUKE 4:18–19 AND THE SECULAR SPIRITUAL SYMBOL OF *LA RAZA CÓSMICA*

La Raza Cósmica is a secular symbol with spiritual overtones. Vasconcelos tells us that "it is necessary that the Iberoamerican race comprehend its mission and embrace it like a mysticism."[9] This race also has to be more capable of true brotherhood and of a vision truly universal.[10] The mission of *La Raza* is to give rise to people ethnically and spiritually.[11] It is to declare the equality of the whites, Blacks, and Indians on (Hispanic) soil.[12] "And thus a warm and big heart ought to be forming in us which embraces, contains, and affects all itself; but filled with vigor, imposes new laws for the world."[13]

> . . . Jesucristo, the author of the major movement of history, who announced love of all men.
> This love will be one of the fundamental dogmas of the fifth race [*La Raza Cósmica*] which ought to arise in [Latin] America. Christianity liberates and engenders life, because it contains universal revelation, not a national one.[14]

Vasconcelos ought to have said that these qualities apply to all races of people, not just to *La Raza Cósmica*. A Chicano theology must stress this point in going beyond one race because they are *mestizos*: the merger of two races. Vasconcelos continues: If [*La Raza*] should fail to love, it will forfeit its mission of being the seat of a humanity made from all nations and races of people.[15] "Christianity preached love as the base for all human relations and now it is beginning to be seen that only love is capable of producing a sublime humanity."[16]

Vasconcelos was convinced that love had to be the focal point of all human relationships. Only in this manner would humankind or a nation of people achieve a communal sisterhood and brotherhood. Vasconcelos believed that the Hispano race was the fifth race in history because of its *mestizaje*. Such a race was to be all-inclusive, not exclusive of differences. He believed that the union or synthesis of different races would create a strong humanity and not a weak exclusivistic one. Vasconcelos emphasized that *La Raza Cósmica* was a mixture of all races. He also stressed that only in Latin America could this mixture be found. "There in [Latin America] are a thousand bridges for the sincere and cordial fusion of all races."[17] Such a fusion he believed would cause the appearance of the fifth era of the world, the era of universality and of cosmic sentiment.[18] Up to this point Vasconcelos's ideology of *La Raza* is comparable to the Lukan message of the good news. But Vasconcelos added: "Life founded on love will reach to express itself in forms of beauty." A Chicano theology must maintain that life founded on love will reach to express itself in forms of justice, equality, and humility. When he speaks about the third level of social existence, the aesthetic, his real class sentiments and eugenic models are expressed.[19]

To me this citation leaves the mundane reality out of our existence. It has an underlying meaning that *los pobres* will no longer be with us because through our quest for beauty they will fade away. Within this model exists a hierarchy with the white on the top and the Black at the bottom.[20] This idea is racist. A Chicano theology will not permit it in its use of *La Raza* as a symbolic tool toward liberation.

A similar flaw in this ideology is found in Vasconcelos's explanation of the third racial level in which *La Raza* follows the concept of beauty with a passion. Vasconcelos states:

The ugly will not procreate, nor will they desire to procreate. . . . Poverty, defective education, the scarcity of beautiful types, the misery which causes people to be ugly, all these calamities will disappear from the future states.[21]

Here Vasconcelos contradicts the Lukan message of liberation: *los pobres* do not fade away; they are raised up. In this statement Vasconcelos replaces scientific eugenics with an aesthetic eugenics.[22]

Regardless of racial level, racism is racism. Vasconcelos did not

take a leap of faith and adopt a nonracist model. Since his dialogue
was with eugenicists, this could have been difficult for him. He did
not have the knowledge of race relations that we now have. His
class status could also have prevented him from seeing another
perspective. Whatever the reason, a Chicano theology with its
emphasis on Luke 4:18–19 cannot accept beauty as the criterion for
promoting the Kingdom of God on earth. For a Chicano theology,
racism is evil and must be overcome by nonracist models. Our oral
tradition provides us with some of these models: cosmicity, *entre la
gente*,[23] *mestizaje*, hope, and *liberación*.

LA RAZA CÓSMICA: ITS SIGNIFICANCE
AND ITS AMBIGUITIES

La Raza Cósmica is an important symbol for Chicanos because
of its theory of inclusivity. It provides us with many positive
attitudes about ourselves including the emphasis on our identity.

Inherent in the symbol of *La Raza* are potential dangers and
ambiguities. Vasconcelos (chapter 5), fought against racism but
established a hierarchy of white over black in his analysis. In the
Chicano experience lighter Chicanos are favored over darker Chicanos. In giving direction to a Chicano theology, we ought not
overlook this fact. In chapter 5 I also stated that if the evil from
both oppressor and oppressed predominated in *mestizaje*, it would
be a disaster. Only in recognizing the dangers inherent in the symbol
of *La Raza* can we guard against them. No symbol is exempt from
possible misuse. It is in recognizing the process of liberation that we
can give these symbols a healthier direction.

As with the symbol of Guadalupe, Chicano leaders who recognize the process of liberation can use the symbol of *La Raza*
to strengthen in the people the impulse to break those chains
of oppression that keep them terrorized. A Chicano theology
must admit the dangers and ambiguities inherent in the symbol
and then give direction to reconstruct and re-create more humanizing models of liberation. In giving direction to a Chicano
theology the symbol of *La Raza* can be used to denounce the
evils of racism and to announce the era of a new humanity in
which color is not a determining factor for superiority or inferiority.

ROLES OF GUADALUPE AND *LA RAZA CÓSMICA* IN DEVELOPING A CHICANO THEOLOGY OF LIBERATION

Guadalupe Within Folk Catholicism

Catholicism plays a major role in Chicano culture. Chicano attitudes are also formulated by their Catholic tradition. But this tradition is a folk Catholicism. The Catholic faith and folk Catholicism are interwoven into the culture so that it is difficult to separate one from the other. Guadalupe as the symbol of symbols in folk Catholicism is the glue (Tomás Atencio) that holds and ties everything together. Guadalupe is a symbol of *re-ligare*. She ties us back to our cosmic center, to our cultural roots. As a symbol of a nurturing mother, she represents the center of our sacred and secular space and time.

Tomás Atencio tells us: "Symbols are the only things that are going to tie us to the global community. Myth is basically energy."

This energy in Guadalupe gives a Chicano theology of liberation cosmic dimension. Through Guadalupe's energy, cosmos is created out of chaos. Guadalupe's energy ties us to the global community by giving us our identity (who we are), by helping us to formulate our meaning structures (what we stand for and what we will die for), and by forming relationships (what we have and share in common with others). Guadalupe in Chicano liberation is a threat to the affluent and the superpowers because she is symbolic of the Chicano poor. She takes care of us.

> No one who seeks me with a genuine need or affliction will turn away unconsoled. No tear will escape my pity. No smallest sigh will go unheard.[24]

Guadalupe consoles and takes pity on the oppressed. She is the symbol of Mexico and its poor. All the great religions of the world have one thing in common with Guadalupe: among their followers the greatest number are poor. Guadalupe, like other great religious symbols, is faith and hope for millions of poor people. When *concientización* occurs among the people the symbols that give the meaning structures to peoples' existence take their place by the side

of the oppressed.[25] In their struggle toward liberation their religious
and national symbols are viable phenomena for their theology. In
this sense Atencio is correct: Guadalupe for Chicanos becomes the
glue that ties us in to the global community. Since most of the global
community is impoverished and Guadalupe is the "liberator of the
oppressed" other suffering humanity will understand our struggle
by understanding the role that Guadalupe plays in our experience
of oppression. By a common understanding of our symbols, we
will share in common struggle to find solutions to causes of oppression from whatever source. Global consciousness will come from
our unity in affliction. Our unity in affliction will give rise to our
unity in liberation.

If we can tie the traditional roles of folk Catholicism to a
theology of liberation and to the social sciences, we will have a
powerful intellectual tool to understand and to be understood by
the world community (Tomás Atencio). I believe Chicanos can
develop a theology from their own perspective, just as others have
developed theologies from their own experiences of oppression.
The different new movement for us will not be to become rich and
powerful and overcome power, but rather to become brothers and
sisters whose dominant theological model will be to bring down the
rich and mighty and raise up the lowly and hungry. This may sound
utopian, but it is not. Our Chicano experience exemplifies that.
Here we are, the product of an actual historical event.

La Raza Cósmica as a Secular-Spiritual Symbol of Sisterhood and Brotherhood

Living in a racist situation, it is easy to fall into the tragic flaw of
racism just as Vasconcelos did and as anyone does who writes from
an experience where racism prevails. Traditional attitudes have
blended racism into the woodwork of our experience. Racism is evil
because it creates a social phenomenon where a superior exists over
an inferior. Racism is a sin against human dignity.

In order to promote a healthy and just society the idea of
brotherhood and sisterhood ought to be stressed. *La Raza Cósmica*
is an attempt at that social vision. As a *mestizaje*, *La Raza* ought
not to suffer from racial prejudices. *Mestizos* backed up by their
cultural Catholic tradition and by their indigenous roots are racial
mixtures. Their existence in the Americas proves that *mestizaje*

does work. The symbol of *La Raza* is important because it names who we are as *mestizos*. We call ourselves *La Raza*. That is who we are. Blacks call themselves Black in their process toward liberation; American Indians call themselves native Americans.

Uno para saber quien es, se dice quien es. Se da su propia identidad [José Ángel Gutiérrez].

"To know who you are, you say who you are. You give yourself your own identity."

All theology in order to be Christian has to be nonracist; otherwise it is not Christian theology. For the Chicano theologian the hidden danger in using the symbol of *La Raza* is the tendency to slip into racism. In doing theology, we must keep this danger in perspective. The simple way out would be not to use the symbol. But the real challenge for the theologian as shown by the Chicano leaders is to address the problem as a complex phenomenon. Only one leader interviewed for this study saw *La Raza* as exclusivistic. Eight saw it as inclusivistic and nonracist. I believe that *La Raza Cósmica* is a symbol that the Chicano theologian must develop in order to understand our process of liberation. The task of Chicano theologians is to be on guard against racism and to extract it from their theology. Chicano theologians see racism as a great obstacle to building the Kingdom of God on earth. The Body of Christ cannot be one, the communion of saints cannot become a reality, if racism is permitted to prevail. Chicano theology takes a strong stance against racism.

La Piel del Problema

Chicanos are caught between two extremes. They are part of the membrane, the skin, that separates impoverished Latin America from affluent North America. As *pochos*, Mexicans from the United States, we are oppressed by Mexicans. As Chicanos we are oppressed by gringos. We feel the *golpes* (sharp pains) from two sides. Yet a theology from such a political position will be advantageous. We understand the gringo impulse and we sympathize with the oppressed of Latin America because our warmth, sincerity, and *corazón* comes from there.

A theology from such a position will give insight into both

cultures. It will be a bridge, a meeting point, between two opposites. This is necessary as the two, instead of coming closer together, are getting further apart. The concept of *La Raza* is one of inclusivity. We cannot afford to alienate each other any more. The ultimate conclusion to alienation between peoples and nations is nuclear war. A Chicano theology sees this as an inevitable outcome unless some channels of cooperation are opened.

The oppressive experience of being caught in the middle can contribute new insights. Ours cannot be a neutral position; we must take sides with the oppressed. It is like being caught in the crossfire, in the middle of action. There is no room for lukewarmness in a Chicano theology of liberation. If we have to fight our brothers and sisters for justice and for equality of distribution of the world's resources then we are left with no other choice, unless our biblical theology has already realized itself in new action. Our theology must be one of praxis and not one of luxuriating in abstract philosophical and theological concepts of God.

In a Chicano theology, God, Jesus Christ, the Virgin of Guadalupe, and the concept of *La Raza Cósmica* show us how to be Christians. Instead of asking what is a Christian, who is a Christian, when are we Christians, why are we Christians, we are Christians by following the precepts of Jesus Christ: loving our neighbor as we love ourselves. Instead of preaching, now we practice. Instead of praying for our salvation, we pray for the liberation of the oppressed.

The role of faith in a Chicano theology is to worry about the needs of those who suffer, with priority given to those who suffer the most. Faith moves mountains because no obstacle is great enough to shake the belief that Jesus will take care of us if we care for his little ones. Chicano theology is pre-Constantinian in its christocentric worldview. The Christian does not compromise with the state at the expense of the oppressed. Growers, agribusiness, and wealthy families in the United States and privileged party members in the Union of Soviet Socialist Republics cannot compromise the oppressed and expect to represent the welfare of humankind. Faith is the strength and courage to say no when others say yes. Faith is revolutionary only when it goes against the status quo that legitimizes the existence of the oppressed. Prayer in a Chicano theology has to be creative in destroying old models of oppression, but visionary and cosmic in creating new models of liberation. Prayer that has no deeds to its spiritual account is worthless.

To sum up the role of symbols in the development of a Chicano theology of liberation, I am reminded of something Bernard Cooke said:

> Genuine myth is an imaginative expression of an insight into the causative structures of existence, an insight that is deeply philosophical though not formulated in philosophical language.

Both Guadalupe and *La Raza Cósmica* give us an insight into the causative (meaning) structures of existence (our cosmic experience of oppression). Their significance is that they show how our bodies are shaped in historical racial strife and how our spirit can be and is alive with energy, life, and hope. Both exemplify a theory of merger, but of dignity in the midst of the struggle.

ESSENTIAL ELEMENTS OF A CHICANO THEOLOGY
OF LIBERATION

Through my investigation, I discovered important and essential elements of a Chicano theology of liberation. The investigation, as stated in chapter 3, was conducted by means of personal interviews in which Chicano leaders were all asked questions or asked to respond to statements on themes affecting the Chicano community.

The Themes

The theme "*Machismo y La Mujer*" I borrowed from Rev. Leo D. Nieto's article "The Chicano Movement and the Churches in the United States."[26] The theme's importance stems from the central role and esteem women are given in Chicano culture. Paradoxically Chicanas suffer oppression because of *machismo* attitudes. Both women interviewed addressed this issue directly.

From my own experience and observations I chose the theme "Racism-Classism." In the United States most peoples of color suffer because of racist attitudes on the part of the dominant white

Anglo-Saxon culture. These attitudes force most Chicanos to exist on the social, economic, and political periphery of North American human existence.

The theme "Education and Labor" I also took from my own experience. Early in life Chicanos in the inner city are encouraged to get a good education in order to get a good job. Chicanos have discovered that in most instances an education does not necessarily lead to such a job. "Violence and Nonviolence" was another theme that I chose from my own experience and from reading about Chicanos in violent and nonviolent struggles toward our liberation. César Chávez's farm workers' nonviolent movement had a great influence on my decision to select this theme.[27]

El respeto al derecho ajeno es la paz, "Respect for the rights of others is peace," a saying by a famous president of Mexico, Benito Juárez, was chosen because of the frequency of its use in the *barrios* of the Southwest. I consider "The Land" as very important to our identity and destiny as a people. Historically, we have been colonized and treated as strangers in our land. The theme "Fatalistic and Anarchistic Tendencies" I borrowed from Rev. Leo D. Nieto. Chicanos have always been accused of showing these tendencies. I decided to develop this theme further by presenting it to our leaders. The themes of "The Catholic Church" and "Theology" are mine. I chose them from my readings and my own experience. Both will play an important role in our future as Chicanos in the United States.

The Symbols

The symbol of Exodus I selected because most liberation movements in Africa and Latin America have addressed this theme. For oppressed peoples this theme is very important. The Religious Symbol of Guadalupe was chosen because of its impact on our Chicano culture. Historically Guadalupe has been used both to legitimize institutionalized oppression against our people and also to strengthen our struggles toward liberation. This theme is important because almost every Catholic Chicano home venerates Guadalupe and beseeches her intercession.

Finally I chose the Secular-Religious Symbol of *La Raza Cósmica* as a major theme because of its importance to our identity as *mestizos. La Raza* is an inclusive term for all Latin Americans. It is also a powerful symbol for uniting Chicanos, Hispanos, and other Latin Americans in this hemisphere toward social, economic, political, and spiritual liberation.

Differences between the Chicano Leaders

Both of the women I interviewed are strong believers, but they are critical of the church when it neglects the issues of women in society. The two Protestant men I interviewed believe that the church is a last hope for Chicanos in the Southwest. They felt, as did three others, that the church could be a sacrament of liberation. Two of the men felt that the church had sided with the oppressors. Of these two, one felt that the church is so culpable that it could under no circumstances be trusted. He did admit, however, that in Latin America there were priests and nuns who were exceptional human beings because they sided with the oppressed. He could trust them because their deeds spoke louder than their words.

Six of the Chicano leaders were willing to compromise on pertinent issues in order to achieve liberation for Chicanos. Three were not willing to compromise because they felt the deck was stacked against Chicanos. Six were for nonviolence and three were for whatever means was necessary to achieve our liberation. On the question of European theology, all agreed that it excluded Chicanos and other oppressed peoples in its perspective.

All except two agreed that the issue of the land is still an open question. All agreed that the symbols of Guadalupe and *La Raza Cósmica* would be significant in developing a Chicano theology of liberation. On the religious symbol of Exodus in relationship to our liberation, two gave a new meaning and a new light to our situation. Unlike the Hebrews who were oppressed in a foreign land, Chicanos are oppressed in their own land.

Findings of Value for a Chicano Theology of Liberation

All those interviewed agreed that Chicanos are oppressed and ought to struggle toward liberating themselves from those enclaves of poverty and misery that maintain their status as inferiors and nonbeings in a system that exploits their labor and culture. Besides the physical chains that keep us oppressed, liberation must also include breaking the spiritual and psychological chains of bondage. The consensus was that our struggle ought to align itself with the Third World. As to the method of liberation, there was no consensus on violence or nonviolence. Six opted for nonviolence and three for whatever means necessary.

All the leaders agreed that the church is not doing all it could for Chicanos. Even those who see the church as an institution working against Chicano liberation believe the church is the last hope for Chicanos. They all also expressed the need for the church to preserve the language, traditions, and identity and culture of Chicanos. Chicanos have a strong identity with the land. Education has meant assimilation into a dominant culture, hence this is a problem. Education does not usually mean humanization but rather alienation from Chicano culture. Emphasis on education is not the same in Chicano culture as in Anglo or Black culture. Some Chicano leaders pointed out that an education was not necessary for success.

The church has much homework ahead to overcome *machismo*. It was stressed that much of the *machismo* in Chicano culture can be traced to the church's attitudes toward the inferiority of women. For Chicanos, as for Blacks in the United States, race as an issue takes precedence over class.

Fatalism and anarchism are not necessarily negative attitudes for Chicanos. Judging from our experience of oppression Chicanos see positive elements in both to insure our survival. It was emphasized that the Exodus theme can apply to Chicanos psychologically and spiritually but not physically. Chicanos are colonized and oppressed in their *own* land. If the Exodus theme were to be stressed, it would be interpreted that we are strangers in our own land. We are not. This is our land.

In our struggle toward liberation, Chicanos relate to an impoverished world and its needs. Chicanos are a bridge between the rich and the poor nations. Because of this ability to be a bridge, the findings stressed that if Chicanos struggle successfully toward liberation, we will have the potential and capability to be a hope for this hemisphere, divided as it is into the oppressors from the North and the oppressed from the South.

Theological Insights Derived from Chicano Experience

DEFINING THEOLOGY. Theology is the study of God by men and women in their relationship to other persons. Theology forces the question: How do we know or love God, if we do not first know or love the neighbor, "the other"? We cannot separate theology from the experience of a people. Experience, lived reality, is part of the ongoing process of creation and men and women's constant struggle and dialogue with it.

The Chicano cosmic experience is one of oppression. A Chicano theology must reflect on the process of liberation. In this process it must re-invent, re-create, re-define, and re-construct in its proper context by drawing on its own proper reality. In its vision it must search for an experience of liberation; this demands that we re-create new models to help us understand the oppressed-colonized context out of which we think, speak, and love. Therefore, we cannot insert old models into new situations of liberation. We must let go of the old man/woman, as St. Paul exhorts us, and take on the new man/woman. These models ought to be created in the midst of the process of liberation. Our theology has to help us recognize this process. We must envision new models, which come from an experience of oppression moving toward liberation.

The uniqueness of our experience lies in the fact that we exist between two worlds: the impoverished and the rich. In giving direction to a Chicano theology of liberation, Chicanos cannot be neutral. Neutrality in the global setting of rich and poor nations implies a choice. To opt for the poor, I believe, involves a prophetic decision, one that paves the way toward liberation for both oppressed and oppressors.

I believe those who are prosperous and consume most of the world's marketable resources by exploiting Latin American, African, and Asian peoples should maintain a less prophetic position. As the distance between rich and poor grows, the prophetic commitment is to opt for the poor. Chicano theology coming out of the enclaves of oppression finds acceptable the models of liberation from the impoverished nations. Chicano theology ought to align itself with the theologies of liberation from Latin America, Africa, Asia, and North American movements—Black, feminist, Asian, and Native American theologies.

THEOLOGICAL INSIGHTS OF A CHICANO THEOLOGY DERIVED FROM THE COSMIC EXPERIENCE OF OPPRESSION. All the Chicano leaders I interviewed agreed that Chicanos are oppressed. Most agreed that the struggle of the poor nations is also our struggle. A consensus was reached that European theology permitted and sustained our oppression. With its foreign concepts and impositions it failed to address the racist conditions that legitimized our conquest and sustained our colonized oppression into the twentieth century. It did not take into consideration our *mestizaje*, our culture, our language, and our dignity as human beings. In short it left us out; we became an invisible people wandering as foreigners and aliens in our own land. Even our church abandoned us. Only our poverty, our communion, the grace of God, and Our Lady of Guadalupe helped us to survive.

Out of this reality Chicanos will have to insist on their theology recognizing the process of liberation. This theology will have to introduce the concept of *mestizaje*. We have been discriminated against and considered inferiors because of our mixture of two races: the Spanish and the native American. Chicano theology must take a new positive direction by using *mestizaje* symbolically to reinforce our identity and our positive cultural attributes. This will have to be done in the same way that the word "Black," once negative and derogatory, was symbolically given a positive and liberative meaning by Black leaders.[28] Our Chicano leaders have to redirect the phenomenon of *mestizaje* toward strengthening our identity, toward letting the phenomenon give rise to our struggle for equality and dignity. No one can do this for us; we must do it ourselves, as Ricardo Sánchez emphasized.

Another element of our experience: Chicanos are *la piel* (skin) where the rich world (the United States) meets the poor world (Mexico). The theological insight is that since we are caught in the middle our experience can serve as a vehicle for dialogue. We are the juncture point at which the two worlds meet. We are a bilingual, bicultural people who have a *corazón latino* with a gringo impulse. Our theology will have to re-create, re-invent new models, new ways in which the rich nations and the poor nations can communicate with each other. Because we are close to both worlds, new avenues and new visions for a theology can be re-created from our unique political position provided we see the process of liberation going on around us. Our theology will have to address this paradoxical phenomenon by re-creating and introducing viable political alternatives to a capitalism that sustains itself by exploiting large masses of non-white and even some white peoples in the United States.

It was the consensus of all the Chicano leaders that we are treated as strangers and foreigners in our own land. From this reality a liberation theology of the land needs to be introduced, which will begin a dialogue between communal ownership and private ownership of land. Our theology must stress our visibility, integrity, and dignity on our own land. Chicanos have communal land grants, which according to the Treaty of Guadalupe-Hidalgo guarantee that large sections of the Southwest are legally ours. A Chicano theology must stress that according to the treaty and our native American ancestry, especially in the Southwest, Chicanos were here first, as Professor Rubén Armendariz stated in our study. A Chicano theology of liberation will have to support our right to be natives and not foreigners. As Monsignor Longinus Reyes reminded us, "Land is important because it is tied to the psychological identity and spiritual vision of a people." Take the land away and you destroy a people.

In our study education has usually meant assimilation into a dominant culture. This has been a problem. The manner in which this phenomenon has been manipulated by those wishing to preserve the status quo has alienated the Chicanos from their own culture and self-identity. Often the educational system has reinforced our inferiority complex and thus has strengthened the colonizers' grasp of our minds. The educational system has only permitted the exceptional Chicano child to achieve. Consequently, for Chicanos, the traditional educational system has been a failure for most of our people.

Theologically speaking, Chicanos must look for some alternatives for strengthening our history, culture, language, and dignity as human beings. The church is one vehicle we can utilize provided we see the process of liberation going on concerning education. Dolores Huerta said that Chicanos who did get an education usually became alienated from the oppressed Chicano community. In theological terms this is devastating to our people. As young leaders get a higher education, they are forced to leave their barrios, cities, and even states. This leaves our oppressed Chicanos without native leadership. There is a need to organize or institutionalize endeavor to move this leadership back into the barrios of the Southwest.

For Chicanos education should mean more than making money and moving ahead competitively. It should mean growth in respect for self and for others. It should mean defending Chicanos. Those Chicanos less fortunate and with less opportunity available to them should be the first on the list. For Chicanos education is not something only material, it is also spiritual. Education for us means to move in the direction of knowing and understanding human relationships. This is where we are strong as a conquered people.

The phenomenon of *La Raza Cósmica* has its roots here. Our theology has to address the human relationship issue in our educational process and give it a dynamic direction for the benefit of both oppressed and oppressors. We can do this provided our leaders see the process of liberation going on and can convey it to our people. A Chicano theology of liberation can give direction to our endeavors by opening up alternative directions to education through such a method as that outlined in Paulo Freire's *Pedagogy of the Oppressed* (see bibliography).

In the area of *machismo*, the study brought out that not only Chicanos struggle against it but that their church must also struggle against it because it makes women subservient to males. A Chicano theology of liberation stresses for Chicanos that their church must not only preach equality, it must also put it into practice. Monsignor Reyes told us in the study that it is the women who strengthen the church in Latin America. Among Chicanos in North America, I suspect the same is true. Yet, in North America the church has much homework to do in this area. We cannot say, "Lord, Lord," and still practice *machismo*. This is not good theology.

In regard to race and class, a Chicano theology emphasizes race over class in North America. In this we are together with our Black and our native American brothers and sisters. A future direction for a Chicano theology of liberation must be toward a comprehensive analysis of racism and a formidable enterprise into possible solutions. The theology of the Magnificat and a theology of prayer will help give us the necessary courage and strength that we need to combat this disease. Chicano theology must help to re-create, re-invent, re-structure new models that are nonracist and all-inclusive of human beings.

For Chicanos, fatalism and anarchistic tendencies are not necessarily negative attitudes. Often we as a conquered people have had to resort to these in order to survive. A Chicano theology suggests that as the process of liberation goes on, more critical analysis into these two phenomena ought to be undertaken. Just because the dominant culture sees both of these as negative does not imply that from our worldview and reality they are necessarily negative for us. If they have helped us to survive thus far, there must be something positive in them. A Chicano theology can give us some insight into re-seeing, re-interpreting, and re-directing our own experienced reality.

Our findings also showed that liberation involves the physical, psychological, and spiritual dimensions of the human person. A Chicano theology of liberation needs to give some positive direction to the concept of liberation. It must initiate a critical process to investigate theologically why we are oppressed. The human sciences will be an important asset to this process. Our theology must borrow and look into these. It must share and align itself with the other liberation theologies that are already in the process of critical analysis, searching for solutions and working toward praxis. It must see itself leaning closer to concrete theology as opposed to abstract and transcendental theology. Any theology that does not take the physical and psychological devastation of oppressed people into consideration is not really in their service. Our study brought this out in regard to Chicanos who do not have a theology that serves their needs as an oppressed community.

As for violence and nonviolence, most of the Chicanos I interviewed, six out of nine, opted for nonviolence. Three opted for any means necessary. A Chicano theology of liberation, I believe, will have to opt for nonviolence. Nonviolence has a creative force that baffles evil. The oppressors are experts at violence and torture, especially the torture of impoverishment—physical and psychological. Often the oppressors "get away" with the torture of the spirit. I believe this could be interpreted as the sin against the Holy Spirit of which Scripture speaks. To torture the human spirit through poverty is to go against God because God does not abandon the oppressed in their last recourse, their last hope, their last attempt at human existence. God will not easily forgive those who violate this sacred area.

Hence, a Chicano theology must insist on and caution the oppressor about this sin. It is also our duty as the oppressed to see that we do not fail in the mission of evangelizing the oppressors, or else everything will have been in vain, even the death on the cross. In the tradition of Pascal, Kierkegaard, and Unamuno, Christianity is agony, a paradox, a contradiction, but it is also the only road to salvation, as Christ himself showed us by his example. In giving direction to a Chicano theology of liberation, our theology will not pass judgment on violence used against oppressors in Latin America. Living in a nation that is the cause of much of the social, political, economic, and spiritual devastation of these poor nations puts us in an awkward position concerning making any moral judgment. But we can pass a judgment against our country if it continues to arm and to supply technological warfare materials to military "democratic" regimes in Latin America that are responsible for much murder, rape, and torture.

A Chicano theology will insist that every time an impoverished citizen is murdered, raped, or tortured, we as North Americans are responsible, and we as Chicanos are also victims. A Chicano theology must raise peoples' consciousness to the realization that when violence happens to Latin Americans it also happens to North American Hispanos in a specific way and to Anglos in a general way in North America. A Chicano theology will inform the Chicano leaders who understand the process of liberation going on that they must convey this message to all members of the church and to all citizens of our country. Whatever happens to one member of the Body of Christ happens to all of us.

A Chicano theology of liberation must tell the world today that hunger and poverty—not the Soviet Union—are the greatest enemies of humankind. The geopolitical politics of both the United States and the Soviet Union are directly responsible; and the United States is more responsible because it consumes more of the world's material resources.

A Chicano theology of liberation will alert everyone to the fact that both West and East provide the arms for impoverished nations to fight against each other. With our history of economic devastation in Latin America, a Chicano theology needs to question whether we are protecting democracy and human dignity in Latin America or protecting our own interests and our multinationals. We are back to Bartolomé de las Casas: Are these not humans? Do they not have rational souls? Are we not to treat them as human beings?

Finally in our study we discovered that the church is not doing all it could do for Chicanos, but it is our last hope. A Chicano theology of liberation will attest to this reality of the church's responsibility. The colonial devastation against Chicanos in the Southwest and the statistics point out our social and economic condition and our dependency complex. The church as an instrument of liberation is our last hope. A Chicano theology needs to give direction to our church leaders provided they see the process of liberation going on. As responsible moral entities, we must cooperate in re-directing and re-structuring a just society for humanity.

Notes

CHAPTER 1. A BRIEF HISTORY OF CHICANOS

1. By *gringo* I mean those foreigners who want to impose the doctrine of Manifest Destiny and will stop at nothing to achieve this. By *Anglo* I mean those foreigners who sympathize with the oppressed.

2. See Elizondo, *Mestizaje*. Chapter 1 gives an excellent treatment of *mestizaje* and its origins in Europe.

3. Hanke, *Bartolomé de Las Casas*, 15.

4. Ibid., 19.

5. Ibid., 20.

6. Lasseque, 78. Lasseque took this information from Bartolomé de Las Casas, *Historia de Las Indias*, book III, chaps. 4–5. I have translated it literally in order to preserve the impact of the content of the sermon.

7. Ibid.

8. Hanke, *Bartolomé de Las Casas*, 21.

9. Ibid., 20.

10. Steiner and Valdez, 33.

11. Ibid., 43.

12. See Las Casas, *Del único modo*.

13. Meier and Rivera, 70.

14. To be developed in chapter 2.

15. The situation of native Americans in the United States is a living reminder to the world of what happens to a conquered population when a powerful nation dishonors its treaties.

16. Romero, 2.

17. Ibid., 19.

18. Ibid.

19. Ibid.

20. Ibid., 20.

21. Ibid., 13.

22. Ibid., 14.

23. Ibid.

24. Ibid.

25. Ibid., 20.

26. See p. 9 of Romero's monograph concerning the guarantee of Martínez's faculties. Note *por el tiempo de la voluntad*, translated as "for as long as desired."

27. Romero, 28.

28. Ibid.

29. Ibid., 28. Quoted from Fray Angélico Chávez, O.F.M., *Archives of the Archdiocese of Santa Fe: Martínez to Lamy*, October 21, 1857.

30. Ibid., 29.

31. Romero, 29. Quoted from Paul Horgan, *Lamy of Santa Fe* (New York: Farrar, Straus and Giroux, 1975), 213.

32. Ibid., 30.

33. Ibid., 31.

34. Ibid. Quoted from Angélico Chávez, O.F.M., October 1856.

35. Romero, 32.

36. Ibid. Quoted from Angélico Chávez, O.F.M., April 13, 1857.

37. Romero, 33. Quoted from Angélico Chávez, O.F.M., May 2, 1857.

38. Ibid.

2. THE CHICANO COSMIC EXPERIENCE OF OPPRESSION

1. The ancestry of a number of Chicanos includes that of Sephardic Jews. Many of them settled in northern Mexico, which today includes the American Southwest. Lopes Reies Tijerina, one of the Chicano leaders I interviewed, claims to trace the history of all Hispanos to Jews of the tribes of Ephraim and Manesseh who converted to Christianity in Spain; hence the name Christian-Israelites. When the New World was discovered many Jews converted to Christianity because of the Spanish Inquisition. *La Raza* for Tijerina means the Christian-Israelites who absorbed the indigenous cultures.

2. See chapter 5 below for Vasconcelos's response to the social Darwinists and to the suggestion of Georg Friedrich Nicolai. Chapter 5, n. 8, refers to a "cosmic tendency" of which Vasconcelos was aware. See also p. 30 of his book *La Raza Cósmica*.

3. Vasconcelos, *La Raza Cósmica*, 36.

4. Ibid., 62.

5. Our African roots are twofold. One comes from slavery, a historical phenomenon in the New World. The other comes from a theory claiming that Africans were here before Columbus. It maintains that the features of the Olmec statues are African.

6. Gutiérrez, *Theology of Liberation*, 108. Gutiérrez quotes from "Peace" (no. 16) from the *Medellín Documents*.

7. CELAM, 78.

8. Acuña, *Occupied America*, iii.

9. Ibid., 3.
10. Acuña, *Occupied America* (2d ed.), 16.
11. Ibid.
12. Ibid., 17.
13. See chapter 1.
14. Acuña, *Occupied America* (2d ed.), 413–14.
15. Ibid., 12.
16. *Stranger in One's Land*, 25–26.
17. Carillo, "Chicano," 11.
18. Acuña, *Occupied America* (2d ed.), 20.
19. Ibid., 20. Acuña quotes from Walter Prescott Webb, *The Great Plains* (New York: Grosset and Dunlap, 1931), 125–126.
20. Burma, 110. Quoted from "The Invisible Minority," *NEA-Tucson Survey on the Teaching of Spanish-Speaking* (Washington, D.C., 1966), 103.
21. Ibid.
22. Ibid., 112.
23. Elizondo, "A Challenge," 164.
24. Carillo, "The Chicano," 11.
25. Hurtado, 189.
26. Anguiano, "Program Overview," 7. Lupe Anguiano is one of the Chicana women I interviewed.
27. Ibid.
28. Tijerina, 75.

3. SHARED THEMES OF THE CHICANO COSMIC EXPERIENCE OF OPPRESSION

1. For a fuller description of this method see Robert Coles's article "The Method" in *Explorations in Psychohistory: The Well Fleet Papers*, ed. Robert Jay Lifton with Eric Olson (New York: Simon and Schuster, 1974), 165.
2. Anguiano, "Program Overview," 7. The survey Anguiano conducted showed that Spanish-speaking, Spanish-surname Catholics constitute about 75 percent of the total Catholic population in the Southwest.
3. Anguiano, "World Women's Challenge," 37.
4. Lernoux, 138.
5. "Their home was my home."
6. This *dicho*, or Chicano proverb, is found among Chicano Texans. It means that all in the family are to be treated equally with no exception.
7. People who in some way are tied to the land.
8. That is the will of God, if that is what God wants, he/she was already destined.

9. Anarchy as understood in the Chicano community is not exclusivistic. It would go against our symbolic identity of *La Raza* if we adhered to a strict anarchism. In order to survive we have had to be both communal and independent. We are communal with one another, but independent when forced to adopt foreign intrigue because of conquest. We may be criticized from the outside for anarchistic tendencies but in reality we are protecting ourselves. In trying to protect our culture, our language, our persons, our religion, and our land, we find it difficult to be communal with gringos who continue their history of oppressing us. Because of oppression, anarchism as seen through Chicano eyes does not have the same meaning as it does in the dominant Anglo-Saxon culture. For us it has positive attributes that have helped us to survive in a hostile milieu.

10. The *Penitentes* is a secret religious-secular society whose roots are in northern New Mexico.

11. This may sound ambiguous, but this is what I mean by a universal partial totality: Traditionally the powerful white West has excluded the mind and ideas of the oppressed. Thus whites are universally partial to themselves and their totality is incomplete and exclusive.

12. *Atzlán* is the name the Aztecs had for the American Southwest before their migration to the Valley of Mexico. Chicanos adopted this pre-Columbian name in the 1960s for the Southwest.

4. THE RELIGIOUS SYMBOL OF GUADALUPE

1. Behrens, 58.
2. Ibid.
3. Ibid.
4. Behrens, 18. Behrens traces this information to Antonio Valeriano, who wrote about Guadalupe around 1560. She tells us that at this time he was an instructor in the Imperial College of the Holy Cross in Tlaltelolco. The original is in Nahuatl. See also Behrens, 14.
5. Behrens, 14.
6. A cloak fastened at the shoulder by a knot.
7. Behrens, 26.
8. Ibid., 27. Behrens quotes from *Breve estudio historico-etimológico acerca del vocablo Guadalupe* by J. Ignacio Davila Garibi.
9. Ibid.
10. Ibid., 29.
11. "Liberator of oppressed races." This title was given to Guadalupe by Don Ezequiel A. Chávez in 1946 in his book *Apuntes autobiográphicos*. See Ezequiel A. Chávez, "La Evangelización de los indios" (58), in *Figuras y episodios de la historia de México*, ed. Alfonso Junco (Mexico: Editorial Jus, S.A., 1958), 30.

12. "The system has swallowed them up."

13. Cox, *Seduction*, 118.

14. Ibid., 118–19.

15. "When oppression has reached its saturation point."

16. Lowry, 10. Quoted from Mircea Eliade, *The Sacred and the Profane: The Nature of Religion*, trans. Willard R. Track (New York: Harcourt, Brace and World, 1959), 32–34.

17. Lowry, 11.

18. See chapter 6, "Conclusions and Perspectives."

19. Paz, 77.

20. "The male mistreats her, beats her, badmouths her, and puts her down."

21. Paz, 72.

5. THE SECULAR-RELIGIOUS SYMBOL OF *LA RAZA CÓSMICA*

1. Nicolai, vii (translator's preface).

2. Ibid.

3. Nicolai, 300.

4. Vasconcelos, *Indologías*, 136.

5. Nicolai, 356.

6. Vasconcelos, *La Raza Cósmica*, 63.

7. Ibid., 9.

8. Hofstadter, 180. Hofstadter quotes John Hays's meaning of "cosmic tendency": "No man, no party, can fight with any chance/of final success against a cosmic tendency,/no cleverness, no popularity awaits the spirit of the age."

9. Hofstadter, 172–73.

10. Ibid., 177. Hofstadter quotes from Fiske's *American Political Ideas*, 135.

11. Ibid., 179.

12. Ibid., 178.

13. Ibid., 171–72. Hofstadter quotes Julius W. Pratt in "The Ideology of American Expansionism," *Essays in Honor of William E. Dodd* (Chicago, 1935), 344.

14. Nicolai, 353.

15. "Heart of *La Raza*": the heart implies sympathy, warmth, soul, affection toward others.

16. See chapter 6, "Conclusions and Perspectives," for further clarification.

17. Gutiérrez's statement is difficult to translate. He means that Chicanos are caught between two political and economic poles—Mexico and the

United States. Chicanos are the first to feel all aspects of the oppression because they live in the United States.

6. CONCLUSIONS AND PERSPECTIVES

1. Boesak, 20–21.
2. Francisco Soto C., "El Nican Mopohua: Nota Bibliográfica," *SER-VIR: Teología y Pastoral* 95–96 (1981):424.
3. Brown, et al., 141.
4. Ibid., 142.
5. Rubén R. Dri, "El Mensaje Liberador Guadalupano," *SERVIR* 95–96 (1981):302.
6. McKenzie, 684. To gain greater depth of the Christian meaning of *los pobres*, McKenzie's entire section on "Poor and Poverty" ought to be read.
7. Ibid., 682.
8. Ibid., 681–82. "ANET" refers to Pritchard, *Ancient Near Eastern Texts*.
9. Vasconcelos, *La Raza*, 36.
10. Ibid.
11. Ibid., 34.
12. Ibid.
13. Ibid., 38.
14. Ibid., 56.
15. Ibid., 57.
16. Ibid., 58.
17. Ibid., 35.
18. Ibid., 57.
19. Ibid., 46.
20. Ibid., 43, 52.
21. Ibid., 50.
22. Ibid.
23. "Among the people": Gutiérrez tells us that this indigenous concept belonged to the native American who knew only one race. In that milieu, dichotomies and hierarchies due to race did not exist.
24. Eliot, 7.
25. The word *concientización* is borrowed from Paulo Freire. See his book *Pedagogy of the Oppressed*, 19–21.
26. Nieto, "Chicano Movement," 32.
27. César Chávez is president of the United Farm Workers of America, AFL-CIO.
28. Aimé Césaire, *Discourse on Colonialism*, trans. Joan Pinkham (New York: Monthly Review Press, 1972), 74.

Glossary

academia: academy

altares: little altars

amistades: friendships

Aztlán: Chicano name for the U.S. Southwest; legendary origins of the Aztec migration to the Valley of Mexico

casa: home

catolicismo popular: popular Catholicism, folk Catholicism

Chicanos: *pachuco* term of self-dignity, self-identity, and self-reliance adopted by militant Mexican grandparents, parents, and youth born, raised, and mistreated in the United States

comadre: godmother; extended family

compadrazgo: closely knit, extended family relationships lasting for life

compadre: godfather; extended family

concientización: process of becoming aware of reality, acting critically upon it, and setting out to liberate it and re-create it

corazón: warmth; love; heart; sympathy

dicho: a saying; a proverb

Dios: God

el campo: the outdoors; the fields

encomendero: Spanish *patrón* to whose care native Americans were entrusted

encomienda: system in which the Spanish *patrón* looked out for welfare of native Americans entrusted to him; in most cases a system of human exploitation

gachupín: derogatory name for Spaniard

golpes: institutional pains; sharp blows

gringos: whites who will not tolerate racial and cultural differences

güero: light-skinned

indiado: Indianness; being Indian

indios: native Americans

la gente: the people

la paz: peace

La Raza: the people; the race; the *mestizos*
latino: hispanic; indo-hispanic
la tierra: the land, symbolically a mother for Chicanos
liberación: liberation; freedom; dignity
libertad: freedom; self-reliance
los pobres: the poor; the oppressed
los rinches: the Texas Rangers (a derogatory name)
los ricos: the rich; the oppressors
machismo: male chauvinism
mestizaje: phenomenon of children whose parents are of different races
mestizos: children born of Spanish (white European) father and Indian mother or vice versa
morena: brown or bronze woman
mujer: woman
mulatos: children born of Spanish (white European) father and African mother or vice versa
nuestra tierra: our land, symbolically our mother
pachuco: barrio youth who refuse to be absorbed by the status quo and who have no opportunities within that system
patrón: boss; exploiter
Penitentes: A brotherhood in New Mexico noted for its rituals and practices
piel: skin; membrane
pobrecito: poor; a term of condolence
pochos: derogatory name for Mexicans/Chicanos of the United States
pueblo: people
somos: we are
supersticiosos: superstitious
también: also
trigueño: dark-skinned
vendido: selling out
vida: life; essence
vivos: intelligent; wise

BIBLIOGRAPHY

BOOKS

Abbott, Walter M., S.J., ed. *The Documents of Vatican II*. New York: Guild Press, 1966.

Abrahams, Peter. *Tell Freedom: Memories of Africa*. New York: Alfred A. Knopf, 1971.

Acuña, Rodolfo. *Occupied America: A History of Chicanos*. 2d ed. New York: Harper & Row, 1981.

————. *Occupied America: The Chicano's Struggle Toward Liberation*. San Francisco: Cantfield Press, 1972. (2d ed., 1981.)

Baum, Gregory. *Religion and Alienation*. New York: Paulist Press, 1975.

Behrens, Helen. *America's Treasure: The Virgin Mary of Guadalupe*. Mexico, 1955.

Bellah, Robert N. *The Broken Covenant*. New York: Seabury Press, 1975.

Boesak, Allan Aubrey. *Farewell to Innocence: A Socio-Ethical Study of Black Theology and Black Power*. Maryknoll, N.Y.: Orbis Books, 1977.

Bonhoeffer, Dietrich. *The Cost of Discipleship*. New York: Macmillan, 1963.

————. *Letters and Papers from Prison*. Edited by Eberhard Bethge. New York: Macmillan, 1967.

Brackenridge, R. Douglas, and Francisco O. Garcia-Treto. *Iglesia Presbyteriana: A History of Presbyterians and Mexican Americans in the Southwest*. San Antonio: Trinity University Press, 1974.

Brown, Raymond, et al., eds. *Mary in the New Testament*. Philadelphia: Fortress Press, 1978.

Buber, Martin. *I and Thou*. Translated by Ronald Gregor Smith. New York: Charles Scribner's Sons, 1958.

Burma, John H., ed. *Mexican Americans in the United States: A Reader*. Cambridge, Mass.: Schenkman, 1970.

Camarillo, Albert. *Chicanos in a Changing Society: From Mexican Pueblos to American Barrios in Santa Barbara and Southern California, 1848–1930*. Cambridge: Harvard University Press, 1979.

Cardenal, Ernesto. *The Gospel in Solentiname*. Translated by Donald D. Walsh. Maryknoll, N.Y.: Orbis Books, 1976–82.

Casavantes, Edward J., *El Tecato: Cultural and Sociological Factors Affecting Drug Use Among Chicanos*. Washington, D.C.: National Coalition of Spanish-Speaking Mental Health Organizations, 1976.

Castro, Fidel. *History Will Absolve Me*. London: Jonathan Cape, 1968.

CELAM. *The Church in the Present-Day Transformation of Latin America in the Light of the Council*. Vol. 2, *Conclusions*. Edited by Louis Michael Colonnese. Offical English edition. Bogotá: General Secretariat of CELAM, 1970.

Chávez, Fray Angélico, O.F.M. *Archives of the Archdiocese of Santa Fe, 1678–1900*. Bibliographical Series. Washington, D.C.: Academy of American Franciscan History, 1957.

Clarkson, John F. et al. *The Church Teaches: Documents of the Church in English*. St. Louis: B. Herder, 1955.

Coles, Robert. *Uprooted Children: Early Life of Migrant Farmworkers*. New York: Harper & Row, 1970.

Cone, James H. *Black Theology and Black Power*. New York: Seabury Press, 1969.

———. *A Black Theology of Liberation*. New York: J. B. Lippincott, 1970.

———. *God of the Oppressed*. New York: Seabury Press, 1969.

Cox, Harvey G. *The Secular City*. New York: Macmillan, 1965.

———. *The Seduction of the Spirit: The Use and Misuse of Man's Religion*. New York: Simon and Schuster, 1973.

Daly, Mary. *Beyond God the Father: Toward a Philosophy of Women's Liberation*. Boston: Beacon Press, 1973.

Deloria, Vine J. *Custer Died for Your Sins: An Indian Manifesto*. New York: Avon Books, 1969.

———. *We Talk, You Listen*. New York: Dell Publishing, 1970.

Durkheim, Emile. *The Elementary Forms of the Religious Life*. Translated by Joseph Ward Swain. New York: The Free Press, 1965.

Eliot, Ethel Cook. *Roses for Mexico*. New York: Macmillan, 1940.

Elizondo, Virgilio P. *Christianity and Culture: An Introduction to Pastoral Theology and Ministry for the Bicultural Community*. Noll Plaza, Indiana: Our Sunday Visitor, 1975.

———. *Mestizaje: The Dialectic of Cultural Birth and the Gospel*. I, II, and III. San Antonio: Mexican American Cultural Center, 1978.

———. *La Morenita: Evangelizer of the Americas*. San Antonio: Mexican American Cultural Center, 1980.

Fanon, Frantz. *Black Skin, White Masks*. Translated by Charles Lam Markmann. New York: Grove Press, 1967.

————. *A Dying Colonialism*. Translated by Haskon Chevalier. New York: Grove Press, 1965.

————. *The Wretched of the Earth*. Translated by Constance Farrington. New York: Grove Press, 1967.

Feuer, Lewis, ed. *Marx and Engels: Basic Writings on Politics and Philosophy*. New York: Anchor Press, 1959.

Fiori, Giuseppe. *Antonio Gramsci: Life of a Revolutionary*. Translated by Tom Nairn. New York: Schocken Books, 1973.

Freire, Paulo. *Education for Critical Consciousness*. New York: Seabury Press, 1973.

————. *Pedagogy of the Oppressed*. Translated by Myra Bergman Ramos. New York: Seabury Press, 1974.

Galarza, Ernesto Herman Gallegos, and Julian Samora. *Mexican Americans in the Southwest*. Santa Barbara: McNally and Loftin, 1970.

Gandhi, M. K. *Non-Violent Resistance*. New York: Schocken Books, 1961.

Geffré, Claude, and Gustavo Gutiérrez, eds. *The Mystical and Political Dimension of the Christian Faith*. New York: Herder and Herder, 1974.

Gollin, James. *Worldly Goods: The Wealth and Power of the American Catholic Church, the Vatican, and the Men Who Control the Money*. New York: Random House, 1971.

Gómez, David F. *Somos Chicanos*. Boston: Beacon Press, 1973.

Gonzáles, Rodolfo. *I am Joaquin*. New York: Bantam Books, 1972.

Grebler, Leo et al. *The Mexican-American People: The Nation's Second Largest Minority*. New York: The Free Press, 1970.

Gremillion, Joseph. *The Gospel of Peace and Justice*. New York: Orbis Books, 1976.

Gutiérrez, Gustavo. *Praxis de Liberación y Fe Cristiana*. Colección, Lee y Discute. Series V. No. 48. Madrid: Zero, S.A., Maximo Aguirre, 1974.

————. *A Theology of Liberation*. Translated by Sister Caridad Inda and John Eagleson. Maryknoll, N.Y.: Orbis Books, 1973.

Haley, Alex. *The Autobiography of Malcolm X*. New York: Grove Press, 1965.

Halley, Clifton L. *The Religious Dimension in Hispanic Los Angeles: A Protestant Case Study*. S. Pasadena, Calif.: William Carey Library, 1974.

Hanke, Lewis. *Bartolomé de Las Casas: An Interpretation of His Writings*. The Hague: Martinus Nishoff, 1951.

————. *Las Teorías políticas de Bartolomeo de Las Casas*. Buenos Aires: Instituto de Investigaciones Historicas, 1935.

————. *The Spanish Struggle for Justice in the Conquest of the Americas*. Boston: Little, Brown, 1965.

Häring, Bernard, C.SS.R. *The Liberty of the Children of God.* Translated by Patrick O'Shaughnessy, O.S.B. Staten Island: Society of St. Paul, 1966.

Harrington, Michael. *The Other America: Poverty in the United States.* Baltimore: Penguin Books, 1962.

Hegel, Georg Wilhelm Friedrich. *Reason in History.* New York: Bobbs-Merrill, 1953.

Helps, Arthur. *The Life of Las Casas, "The Apostle of the Indies."* London: Bell and Daldy, 1868.

Hofstadter, Richard. *Social Darwinism in American Thought.* Boston: Beacon Press, 1962.

The Holy Bible. Douay Version. New York: D. and J. Sodliert, 1856.

Horgan, Paul. *Lamy of Santa Fe.* New York: Farrar, Straus and Giroux, 1975.

Hurtado, Juan, *An Attitudinal Study of Social Distance between the Mexican American and the Church.* San Antonio: Mexican American Cultural Center, 1975.

The Jerusalem Bible (JB). New York: Doubleday, 1966.

King, Martin Luther, Jr. *Why We Can't Wait.* New York: New American Library, Signet Books, 1964.

Las Casas, Bartolomé de. *Del único modo de atraer a todos los pueblos a la verdadera religión.* Edited by Augustin Millares Carlo. Panuca, Mexico: Fondo de Cultura Económica, 1942.

————. *In Defense of the Indians.* Edited and translated by Strafford Poole, C.M. De Kalb, Ill.: Northern Illinois University Press, 1974.

Lasseque, Juan B. *La Larga marcha de Las Casas.* Lima: Centro de Estudios y Publicaciones, 1974.

Lernoux, Penny. *Cry of the People.* Garden City: Doubleday, 1980.

Levy, Jacques E. *César Chávez: Autobiography of La Causa.* New York: W. W. Norton, 1975.

Lonergan, Bernard J. F., S.J. *The Subject.* Milwaukee: Marquette University Press, 1968.

Lowry, Shirley Park. *Familiar Mysteries: The Truth in Myth.* New York: Oxford University Press, 1982.

McKenzie, John L., S.J. *Dictionary of the Bible.* Milwaukee: Bruce Publishing, 1965.

McNamara, Patrick H., ed. *Religion American Style.* New York: Harper and Row, 1974.

McWilliams, Carey. *North from Mexico: The Spanish-Speaking People of the United States.* New York: Greenwood Press, 1968.

Madsen, William. *Mexican-Americans of South Texas.* New York: Holt, Rinehart and Winston, 1973.

Marcuse, Herbert. *Counter-Revolution and Revolt.* Boston: Beacon Press, 1972.

Matthiessen, Peter. *Sal Si Puedes: César Chávez and the New American Revolution.* New York: Random House, 1969.

Meier, Matt S., and Felicíano Rivera. *The Chicanos: A History of Mexican Americans.* New York: Hill and Wang, 1972.

Moore, Basil, ed. *The Challenge of Black Theology to South Africa.* Atlanta: John Knox Press, 1974.

Moquin, Wayne, ed. *A Documentary History of the Mexican Americans.* New York: Bantam Books with permission of Praeger Publishers, 1972.

Morales, Armando. *Ando Sangrando.* La Puente, California: Perspectiva Publications, 1972.

Nabokov, Peter. *Tijerina and the Courthouse Raid.* Berkeley: Ramparts Press, 1970.

Neal, Marie Augusta, S.N.D. de N. *A Socio-Theology of Letting Go.* New York: Paulist Press, 1977.

Neihardt, John G. *Black Elk Speaks.* New York: Pocket Books, 1975.

Nicolai, Georg Friedrich. *The Biology of War.* New York: The Century Company, 1918.

Niebuhr, H. Richard. *Radical Monotheism and Western Culture.* New York: Harper and Row, 1960.

Nieto, Leo D. "Christianity and Culture in Mexico." Master's thesis, Texas Christian University, Fort Worth, 1964.

Paz, Octavio. *El Laberinto de la Soledad.* Mexico: Fondo de Cultura Económica, 1973.

Quigley, Thomas E. *Freedom and Unfreedom in the Americas: Toward a Theology of Liberation.* New York: IDOC, 1971.

Rahner, Karl, ed. *Encyclopedia of Theology: The Concise Sacramentum Mundi.* New York: Seabury Press, 1975.

Ricard, Robert. *The Spiritual Conquest of Mexico.* Berkeley: University of California Press, 1966.

Romero, Juan, with Moises Sandoval. *Reluctant Dawn: Historia del Padre A. J. Martínez, Cura de Taos.* San Antonio: Mexican American Cultural Center, 1975.

Rubel, Arthur J. *Across the Tracks: Mexican Americans in a Texas City.* Austin: University of Texas Press, 1971.

Russel, Letty M. *Human Liberation in a Feminist Perspective: A Theology.* Philadelphia: Westminster Press, 1974.

Samora, Julian, ed. *La Raza: Forgotten Americans.* Notre Dame Ind.: University of Notre Dame Press, 1969.

Samora, Julian, Ernesto Galarza, and Herman Gallegos. *Mexican Americans in the Southwest.* Santa Barbara: McNally and Loftin, 1970.

Sánchez, Ricardo. *Canto y grito mi liberación*. New York: Anchor Books, 1973.

Sartre, Jean-Paul. *Anti-Semite and Jew*. Translated by George J. Becker. New York: Schocken Books, 1965.

Segundo, Juan Luis. *The Community Called Church*. Translated by John Drury. Maryknoll, N.Y.: Orbis Books, 1973.

————. *Evolution and Guilt*. Translated by John Drury. Maryknoll, N.Y.: Orbis Books, 1974.

————. *The Hidden Motives of Pastoral Action: Latin American Reflections*. Translated by John Drury. Maryknoll, N.Y.: Orbis Books, 1977.

————. *The Liberation of Theology*. Translated by John Drury. Maryknoll, N.Y.: Orbis Books, 1975.

————. *Our Idea of God*. Translated by John Drury. Maryknoll, N.Y.: Orbis Books, 1974.

Simmen, Edward. *Pain and Promise: The Chicano Today*. New York: New American Library, 1970.

Steiner, Stan. *La Raza: The Mexican Americans*. New York: Harper and Row, 1970.

Steiner, Stan, and Luis Valdez, eds. *Aztlan: An Anthology of Mexican-American Literature*. New York: Alfred A. Knopf, 1972.

Stranger in One's Land. U.S. Commission on Civil Rights. Clearing House Publication No. 17, May 1970.

Thoreau, Henry David. *Walden*. New York: New American Library, 1960.

Thurman, Howard. *Deep River*. Port Washington, N.Y.: Kennikat Press, 1955.

Tijerina, Reies López. *Mi lucha por la tierra*. Mexico: Fondo de Cultura Económica, 1978.

Tolstoy, Leo. *The Kingdom of God Is within You or Christianity Not as a Mystical Teaching but as a New Concept of Life*. Translated by Leo Wiener. New York: Noonday Press, 1961.

Torres, Camilo. *Revolutionary Writings*. New York: Herder and Herder, 1969.

Torres, Sergio, and John Eagleson, eds. *Theology in the Americas*. Maryknoll, N.Y.: Orbis Books, 1976.

Vaillant, G. C. *Aztecs of Mexico*. Baltimore: Penguin Books, 1962.

Vasconcelos, José. *Indología: Una interpretación de la cultura Ibero-Americana*. Paris: Agencia Mundial de Librería, 1927.

————. *La Raza Cósmica: Misión de la Raza Ibero-Americana*. Madrid: Aguilar, S.A. Di Ediciones, 1961.

Weber, Max. *Politics as a Vocation*. Translated by H. H. Gerth and C. Wright Mills. Philadelphia: Fortress Press, 1965.

————. *The Protestant Ethic and the Spirit of Capitalism*. Translated by Talcott Parsons. New York: Charles Scribner's Sons, 1958.

————. *The Sociology of Religion.* Translated by Ephraim Fischoff. Boston: Beacon Press, 1964.

Weiner, Henry N. *The Source of the Human God.* Carbondale, Ill.: Southern Illinois University Press, 1946.

Woods, Donald. *Biko.* New York: Vintage Books, 1978.

ARTICLES

Adams, James Luther. "Theological Basis for Social Action." *The Journal of Religious Thought* 8, 1 (Autumn–Winter, 1950–51): 6.

Anguiano, Lupe. "Program Overview and Annual Report." *Communidad: Southwest Office for the Spanish Speaking* 1, 7 (April–May 1976): 6.

————. "World Women's Challenge: A New Society Based on Justice and Peace." *De Colores: Journal of Emergent Raza Philosophies* 2, 3, Pajarito Publications (1975): 32.

Carrillo, Alberto. "The Chicano and the Church." *IDOC International* (North American Edition, 1972): 10.

————. "The Sociological Failure of the Catholic Church towards the Chicano." *Journal of Mexican American Studies* 1, 2 (Winter 1971): 75.

Castuera, Ignacio. "The Theology and Practice of Liberation in the Mexican American Context." *The Perkins School of Theology Journal* 29, 1 (Fall 1975): 2.

Católicos por La Raza. "Demands." *La Raza* 1, 1 (circa 1971).

Chavarría, Jesús. "La causa Chicana: A Revolution Yet to Come." *Origins NC Documentary Service* 4, 43 (1975): 675.

Chávez, César E. "Blessed are you who hunger and thirst for righteousness; you shall be satisfied." *National Catholic Reporter* 14 (March 7, 1975): 14.

————. "The Mexican American and the Church." *El Grito 1* (Summer 1968): 9.

Cone, James. "Black Theology and the Black Church: Where Do We Go from Here." *Theology in the Americas Documentation Series*, Document No. 4, New York, 1978.

Curti, Josephat. "The Chicano and the Church: Dominant Anglo-Institutions Demand Cultural Suicide and Self-Negation as the Price for Chicano's Acceptance." *Christian Century* 92, 316 (March 12, 1975): 352.

"The Del Rio Mexican-American Manifesto to the Nation." *Maryknoll* 68 (March 1973): 3.

Dworking, Anthony Gary. "Stereotypes and Self-Image Held by Native-Born and Foreign-Born Mexican-Americans." *Sociology and Social Research* 99 (March–April 1965): 214.

Elizondo, Virgilio P. "A Challenge to Theology: The Situation of the Hispanic-Americans." *Catholic Theological Society of America: 1975* Proceedings: 163.

Freire, Paulo. "Education, Liberation and the Church." *Study Encounter.* Geneva: World Council of Churches, 1974.

Gonzales, Justo L. "Searching for a Liberation Anthropology." *Theology Today* 34, 4 (January 1978): 386.

Gutiérrez, Gustavo. "Praxis of Liberation and Christian Faith." Translated from "Praxis de Liberación y Fe Cristiana," in *Signos de Liberación* (Lima: Centro de Estudios y Publicaciones, November 1973): 13.

Hanke, Lewis. "Pope Paul III and the American Indians." *Harvard Theological Review* 3, 2 (April 1937): 97.

Lara-Braud, Jorge. "The Second Largest Ethnic Minority in the USA." *Migration Today* 12 (Spring 1969): 5.

Neal, Marie Augusta, S.N.D. "How Prophecy Lives." *Sociological Analysis* 33 (Fall 1972) 125.

Nieto, Leo D. "The Chicano Movement and the Churches in the United States." *The Perkins School of Theology Journal* 39, 1 (Fall 1975): 32.

———. "Spanish Americans in the Church." *World Outlook* 30, 1 (August 1970): 7.

Salinas, Rudolfo. "The Consistent Inconsistency of the Church." *Con Safos* 2, 5 (1970): 36.

Sandoval, Moises. "Spanish Speaking versus Church." *National Catholic Reporter* (January 17, 1975): 16.

Sylvest, Edwin E., Jr. "The Hispanic-American Church: Contextual Consideration." *The Perkins School of Theology Journal* 29, 1 (Fall 1975): 22.

Theology in the Americas Documentation Series. Document No. 1: "Towards a North American Theology of Liberation: Theology in the Americas Process." New York, 1978.

PAMPHLETS

Guevara, Ernesto ("Che"). *Socialism and Man.* New York: Pathfinder Press, 1968.

Malcolm X (Little). *Talks to Young People.* New York: Pathfinder Press, 1971.

Index

Compiled by William H. Schlau